Reading Group Choices

Selections for Lively Book Discussions

Paz & Associates

2004

For further information, contact:
Mark Kaufman, Editor
Reading Group Choices

Paz & Associates
800/260-8605 — phone
mkaufman@pazbookbiz.com — email

Visit our websites at:
www.readinggroupchoices.com
www.pazbookbiz.com

ISBN 0-9644876-9-1

We wish to thank the authors, agents, publicists, and our publishing colleagues who have continued to support this publication by calling to our attention some quality books for group discussion:

Algonquin Books of Chapel Hill
Ballantine Books (Random House)
Beyond Words
Coffee House Press
Hyperion Books
Middleway Press
Plume Books
Time Warner Book Group
Vintage Books (Random House)
Yale University Press

Anchor Books (Random House)
Beagle Bay Books
Coastal Villages Press
HarperCollins
Louisiana State University Press
Penguin/Putnam Publishing Group
Rodale Books
TOR Books
Writers Club Press
Karen Essex

In appreciation of an ongoing alliance with Paz & Associates and *Reading Group Choices*, we especially thank graphic designer Gena Kennedy for her artwork and production expertise.

INTRODUCTION

Those of you whose book groups have been meeting for 20+ years may wonder why it took the media so long to recognize that book groups are a vibrant part of American culture. Now that television stations and newspapers are sponsoring their own groups, more and more people are reminded of the value of reading—and discovering what a delight it is to belong to a reading discussion group. When we launched *Reading Group Choices* ten years ago, little could we have anticipated just how popular this resource would become—and the fascinating people we'd meet along the way.

From Oprah to *Good Morning America*, from *USA Today* to your daily local newspaper, from "one book, one community" events to an intimate gathering in your living room, book groups have soared to new heights. Though we'll never really know just how many book groups there are or the exact criteria that makes a book a group favorite, we have learned some fascinating tidbits about group members. Would you believe that the average book group participant reads more than 50 books per year? And buys 12 more as gifts for others? We book group members know that books enhance life. Our book group is the perfect place to share thoughts, listen, be open to other ideas, and read things we would never have chosen on our own.

Two years ago we began to compile the Top 20 Favorites List for Book Groups. The list is like having hundreds of book groups in one place, sharing the best books they read during the last year. Will you please let us know your favorites of 2003? Visit us at **www.readinggroupchoices.com** and you'll have the chance to receive free books for each member of your group (compliments of our publishing colleagues) and a $75 check to pay for your refreshments. Please visit the website early in 2004 and again in April when we post the official list.

Now in use at thousands of public libraries and bookstores across the country and thousands more independent book groups, *Reading Group Choices* has become a trusted source for a variety of great reads and discussible books. We're pleased to bring you this tenth anniversary edition and thank you for keeping the world of books alive in our culture.

Mark Kaufman   **Donna Paz Kaufman**

CONTENTS

About Paz & Associates
and *Reading Group Choices*

One of the goals of Paz & Associates is to join with publishers, bookstores and libraries to develop resources and skills that promote books and reading. We offer a variety of products and services, including the following:

◊　consulting with prospective and current retail booksellers—as well as public libraries—on marketing, human resources, design, merchandising, and business operations, including financial analysis, buying and inventory management

◊　*The Reader's Edge* bookstore newsletter marketing program

◊　*Opening a Bookstore: The Essential Planning Guide*

◊　Opening a Bookstore: The Business Essentials, 5-day intensive workshops (see web site for dates and locations)

◊　*The LifeLong Learning Series* and *Training Guide to Front-Line Bookselling*

◊　Training Videos *Exceptional FrontLine Bookselling: It's All About Service* and *Bookstore Merchandising Made Easy*

Reading Group Choices is distributed annually to bookstores, libraries, and directly to book groups. Titles from previous issues are posted on our website at **www.readinggroupchoices.com.** Books presented here have been recommended by book group members, librarians, booksellers, literary agents, publicists, authors, and publishers. All submissions are then reviewed to ensure the "discussibility" of each title. Once a title is approved for inclusion, publishers are then asked to underwrite production costs, so that copies of **Reading Group Choices** can be distributed for a minimal charge.

For additional copies, please call your local library or bookstore, or you may contact us by phone or email as shown below. Quantities are limited. For more information, please visit our websites at **www.pazbookbiz.com** and **www.readinggroupchoices.com**

800/260-860 — dpaz@pazbookbiz.com

THIS YEAR'S
FEATURED TITLES

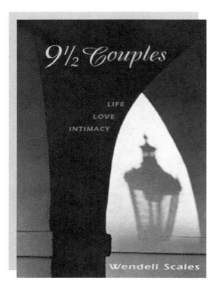

9½ COUPLES

Author: Wendell Scales

Publisher: Capulet House, 2003

Website: www.CapuletHouse
Publishing.com

Available in:
Hardcover, 228 pages. $24.95
(ISBN 0-9728728-0-9)

Subject: Relationships/
Personal Challenges (Fiction)

Summary

9½ Couples takes readers on a journey through the delicate issues that besiege the lives of nine unforgettable couples who—to stay together—must overcome the toughest relationship challenges. It is a story about the intimate and emotional situations and catastrophic changes that result when couples fail to communicate. The story begins with Dr. Jean-Paul Lefervre, a psychiatrist, feeling ineffective and frustrated as a therapist, and guilt-ridden since the death of his wife, Simone. Armed with his new "journal therapy," Jean-Paul is determined to prevent other couples from making the same mistake in their relationships that he made in his. An underlying story emerges as the couples reveal to Jean-Paul their trials with impotence, menopause, infidelity, abuse, forbidden love, and other issues.

Recommended by: Stephani, manager

"This book was a slap of reality. You think reality television is great—READ THIS BOOK!"

Author Biography

Dr. Wendell Scales lives in Michigan. He has maintained a private practice in the Detroit-Metropolitan area for the past twenty-seven years. He has conducted seminars in the Midwest on relationships. He has also written articles on relationship issues for several newspapers. This is his first novel.

Topics to Consider

1) What would drive you into the embrace of another, when you have loving arms waiting to embrace you at home? Would you accept the rationale given by the spouse who cheated? What made the husband ignore the 'silver-haired' woman's advice about a person's eyes?

2) Have you ever been in a May-December relationship? Is this the wave of the future? Which age/gender combination would you say is more likely to last in a relationship of this type?

3) What is it about a forbidden fruit that brings out our most intense feelings of love? What was Dexter's reason for risking his secure and safe haven, for Epiphany's love? Would you risk losing everything to possess a forbidden fruit?

4) You've read about the "Maintenance Man," but have you ever read about the "Transitional Man"? What was the Transitional Man's purpose in the book? Have you ever been a Transitional person?

5) Are you presently in an abusive relationship? Why? What does the 'Stockholm syndrome' have to do with the domestic violence couple in the book?

6) How did your father shape you emotionally? Was he there for you? Was he absent? Do you want to 'dance' with your father again? Did he ever 'dance' with you? If not, do you wish he had 'danced' with you?

7) What, if anything, did you or your male companion do before the release of Viagra to combat impotence? Julia was against taking HRT (hormone replacement therapy): What effect did this have on her marriage to Victor?

8) Can you really compete with a queen of Sheba?

9) What made Julia reject Victor's "South Seas" fantasy? Have you ever been seduced, pampered, thrilled, and satisfied beyond your wildest imagination? Could you handle a Victor, or Victoria?

10) You can forgive a relationship blunder, but can you ever forget it?

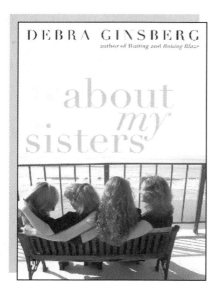

ABOUT MY SISTERS

Author: Debra Ginsberg

Publisher: HarperCollins, 03/2004

Website: www.harpercollins.com

Available in:
Hardcover, 304 pages. $23.95
(ISBN 0-06-052202-X)

Subject: Family/Relationships/
Women's Studies (Nonfiction)

Summary

In *About My Sisters*, Debra Ginsberg examines the bonds of sisterhood through her relationships with her three sisters; Maya, Lavander, and Deja. As their unconventional parents crisscrossed the world in search of the perfect place to live, Debra and her sisters developed a strong and unrestricting closeness as girls that they maintain today as women. Written in the same candid voice that captivated readers in her first two books, *About My Sisters* is an absorbing and heartfelt view into the complex ties of sisterhood.

Author Biography

Debra Ginsberg is the author of *Waiting: The True Confessions of a Waitress* and *Raising Blaze: Bringing Up an Extraordinary Son in an Ordinary World*, both of which have been adopted as texts for creative non-fiction classes and for professional reference. A graduate of Reed College, she is a contributor to NPR's 'All Things Considered' and the *San Diego Union-Tribune* books section.

Topics to Consider

1) Why do you think the author structured the book so each chapter corresponds with a month of the year?

2) How does the relationship the author has with her sisters differ from your relationships with your siblings, or from those of other sisters you know?

3) How much is this truly a "sister" story, and how much a larger "family" story, or really a "memoir" in the traditional sense?

4) The sisters' brother, Bo, makes only cameo appearances, but he's clearly adored by his sisters, and at the same time, given his space. How do you think a man with sisters grows up differently from one who has only brothers, or is any only child?

5) In the author's own words, *About My Sisters* is about the "unbreakable, special bonds of sisterhood as seen through the lives of four sisters." Do you think sisterly bonds are truly unbreakable? What about other kinds of family bonds?

6) The Ginsberg family lives in much closer proximity to one another than many large families in the western world. How do you think physical distance impacts family bonds?

7) Have you ever had the experience of "parenting" a sibling? Do you think it's an inherent responsibility older siblings have for their younger siblings? How does it affect family dynamics?

8) Near the end of the book, while out to eat with her sisters, the author says, "Sisters are always girls, somehow." What do you think she meant? Do you agree?

AMERICAN WOMAN

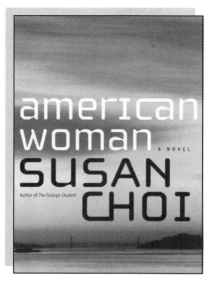

Author: Susan Choi
Publisher: HarperCollins, 2003
Website: www.harpercollins.com
Available in:
Hardcover, 384 pages. $24.95
(ISBN 0-06-054221-7)
Subject: History/Social Issues
(Fiction)

Summary

On the lam for an act of violence against the American government, 25-year old Jenny Shimada agrees to care for three younger fugitives whom a shadowy figure from her former militant life has spirited out of California. One of them, the kidnapped granddaughter of a wealthy newspaper magnate in San Francisco, has become a national celebrity for embracing her captors' ideology and joining their radical cell. Set in the early 1970s, this is a thought-provoking meditation on race, identity, and class. *American Woman* explores the psychology of the young radicals, the intensity of their isolated existence, and the paranoia and fear that undermine their ideals, and features characters based on real radicals of the 1970s. Juan and Yvonne (names and identities altered) were members of the Symbionese Liberation Army who kidnapped Patty Hearst (Pauline in the novel).

Recommended by: *Kirkus Reviews*

"Intellectually provocative and vividly imagined."

Author Biography

Susan Choi was born in Indiana and grew up in Texas. Her short fiction has appeared in several journals, including the *Iowa Review* and *Epoch* magazine. She published her first novel, *The Foreign Student*, in 1998. She lives in Brooklyn, New York.

Topics to Consider

1) What do you feel the author was trying to say in the title, *American Woman*?

2) If you grew up at this time, how does the novel compare to your memory of the Sixties and Seventies? If you were born afterwards, what surprised you most about this time?

3) How might the novel have changed if told from Pauline's point of view?

4) Discuss the many manifestations of love throughout the book. Does Pauline's arrival mark a turn in the novel's eroticism? Why does William continue to evoke such strong emotions in Jenny?

5) Throughout the book we see the characters go through various stages of idealism, disenchantment, revolution and reconstruction. Is this progression universal for all people coming of age or did the time period affect their development?

6) When Jenny comes out of hiding she realizes that the 'newer' radicals have an entirely different view of the world. How do you think age affects one's definition of radical?

7) Throughout American history people have felt called upon to do something to voice their opinions. Do you believe that the actions of violent protestors devalue the endeavors of non-violent people in their efforts to satisfy this need?

8) Are you able to step back and examine how much your beliefs are influenced by the times? Do you think people should adjust their mindset as time progresses or should they hold fast to what they have always thought to be true?

ANYTHING YOU SAY CAN AND WILL BE USED AGAINST YOU

Author: Laurie Lynn Drummond

Publisher: HarperCollins, 02/2004

Website: www.harpercollins.com

Available in:
Hardcover, 288 pages. $23.95
(ISBN 0-06-056162-9)

Subject: Social Issues/
Personal Challenges (Fiction)

Summary

This is a no-holds-barred account of the lives of five female police officers in Baton Rouge, Louisiana. Each woman's story—like each call in a police officer's day—varies in its unique drama, but all the tales illuminate the tenuous line between life and death, violence and control, despair and salvation. These stories reveal how officers are trained to deal with the smell of death, how violence clings to a crime scene long after the crime is committed, how the police determine when to engage in or diffuse violence, why some people make it from the academy to the force and some don't, and all the friendships, romances, and dramas that happen along the way. These stories reveal the humanity, compassion, humor, tragedy, and redemption hidden behind the "blue wall."

Author Biography

Laurie Lynn Drummond's fiction has appeared in such journals as *Southern Review* and *Fiction and Story*, and she was a Tennessee Williams Scholar in Fiction at the Sewanee Writers Conference. She is an assistant professor at St. Edward's University, where she has taught creative writing for the past eleven years. She was formerly a uniformed police officer with the Baton Rouge City Police Department. She grew up in northern Virginia and now lives in Austin, TX.

Topics to Consider

1) If you made an emergency call, would you want a man or woman on the scene, or would it depend what was going on?

2) Police officers perform a vital service for all of us, every day. But in "Katherine's Elegy," Drummond hints at reasons other than altruism for becoming a police officer. Why do you think people become police officers?

3) In this collection, there's only one story - "Keeping the Dead Alive" - in which an all-female group of cops interacts, first socially, then professionally. What does that say about the unique world of the female police officer?

4) From reading her stories, do you think Laurie Lynn Drummond thinks that women approach the job of being a police officer differently than men do?

5) Again and again, Drummond's characters say, or show, that police officers have to rely on gut, on instinct, when assessing a scene and deciding how to act–and there are no second chances. How much of this book do you think is colored by what Drummond would have done differently when she was on the force?

6) One subtitle the publisher considered for this book was "Stories about Women and Guns." Is that an accurate label for this book?

7) The stories in *Anything You Say Can and Will Be Used Against You*, though fictional, are closely based on real events from the author's life, and from the lives of people she worked with as a police officer in Louisiana. Do you think the author had a clear sense of fact and fiction as she wrote?

8) Though cops carry guns day in and day out, in these stories, as in real life, when a cop kills someone or gets killed in the line of duty, it's a big deal. What do you think this says about our society?

THE CAPTAIN'S WIFE

Author: Douglas Kelley

Publisher: Plume, 2002

Website: www.penguin.com

Available in:
Paperback, 304 pages. $14.00
(ISBN 0-452-28355-8)

Subject: History/
Personal Challenges (Fiction)

Summary

Based on the true story of Mary Patten, *The Captain's Wife* begins in July 1856 during the heyday of the great clipper ships. Mary's husband, Captain Joshua Patten, is hired to navigate *Neptune's Car* on a treacherous voyage from New York to San Francisco through one of the most dangerous straits in the Western Hemisphere: Cape Horn. Early on, trouble erupts on the ship. When the first mate is put in chains for plotting a mutiny and the captain falls ill, Mary must take command of the ship. Having learned how to navigate during her last voyage with her husband, Mary is forced to put her skills, authority, and wits to the test as she demands respect from the crew, nurses her husband day and night, and keeps the mutinous first mate at bay.

Recommended by: *Arkansas Democrat-Gazette*

"Kelley's sublime adventure story...will intrigue and delight a generation of readers."

Author Biography

A native of Fort Smith, Arkansas, **Douglas Kelley** now makes his home just across the Oklahoma state line. This is his first novel. Visit *The Captain's Wife* website at **www.TheCaptainsWife.com**.

Topics to Consider

1) Central to the story of *The Captain's Wife* is the relationship between Joshua and Mary Patten. In what ways are the two similar? What are their differences? What do you think makes their relationship work?

2) Why does Wiley encourage Joshua Patten to take on Keeler as his first mate? Is it simply because he needs the ship to sail on time, or does he have some other motive for wanting Keeler on board the *Neptune's Car*?

3) At a time in history where women were thought to be less than equal to men (nearly seventy years before the Nineteenth Amendment would give women the right to vote), Mary Patten surely must have been frustrated by the limitations imposed on her by society. Does her husband also limit, or try to limit, Mary's actions and interests?

4) What, do you suppose, are the reasons for Keeler's actions on board the *Neptune's Car*? Do his motivating intentions change after he learns of Joshua's infirmity?

5) How much credit is due Joshua for quelling Keeler's attempted mutiny? Do you think the outcome would have been different had Mary and Hare had to face down Keeler alone?

6) Fairly given or not, sailors of the era depicted in this novel do not enjoy a historical reputation as the most seemly group of individuals. With this in mind, is it surprising that the majority of the crew follows her lead? Why do they follow Mary's orders?

7) How would you define the relationship forged between Mary Patten and second mate Timothy Hare? Does this relationship change over the course of the novel, and if so, how?

8) Regardless of whether or not she feels she identifies with members of the budding women's movement, is Mary Patten a feminist? Why or why not?

For additional discussion topics, visit www.penguin.com.

THE CENTER OF EVERYTHING

Author: Laura Moriarty

Publisher: Hyperion, 2003

Website: www.hyperionbooks.com

Available in:
Paperback, 304 pages. $15.95
(ISBN 0-7868-8845-8)
Hardcover, 304 pages. $22.95
(ISBN 1-4013-0031-6)

Subject: Family/
Personal Discovery (Fiction)

Summary

Ten-year-old Evelyn Bucknow tries to make sense of an unruly world spinning around her. Growing up with a single mother who is chronically out of work and dating a married man, Evelyn—very often expected to play the role of the adult—learns early how to fend for herself. Readers will find a searing rendering of the claustrophobia of small town midwestern life, as seen through the eyes of a teenage girl. Evelyn must come to terms with the heartbreaking lesson of first love—that not all loves are meant to be—and determine who she is and who she wants to be. Stuck in the middle of Kansas, between best friends, and in the midst of her mother's love, Evelyn finds herself...in *The Center of Everything*.

Recommended by: Robin Vidimos, *Denver Post*

"...Reminds the reader of the full spectrum of youthful experience in all its beauty, anger and pain...lively and endearing."

Author Biography

Since earning her M.A. from the University of Kansas, **Laura Moriarty** won the George Bennet Fellowship for Creative Writing at Phillips Exeter Academy. This is her first novel. She's at work on her next novel and lives in Portland, Maine.

Topics to Consider

1) What do you think of Evelyn, Tina, and Eileen? What about Tina's father? What kind of people are they? What do they look like? What is Sam's role in the family and in the story? Share your impressions of other characters that stand out, and why.

2) Examine and discuss whether or not Evelyn's thoughts and spoken words are reflective of a child's point of view, and why. Share some examples that you find effective and/or moving.

3) How do Evelyn's feelings about her mother affect your feelings about Tina? Explore whether or not you are sympathetic or disgusted by Tina, and why. Share some examples of how Moriarty brings out the mother/daughter relationship and whether or not you can relate to it, and why.

4) What are the roles of friendship pins and particular pieces of clothing in the lives of grade-school kids? What are your memories and experiences of these years? Share whether or not you think Moriarty successfully conveys these school experiences, and why.

5) Discuss the use of religion as a recurring theme throughout the book. As a storytelling device, what purpose does it serve? Why would a man as "religious" as Tina's father shun his daughter and be so unforgiving? How does Eileen live her beliefs? How does religion affect Evelyn?

6) Why does Moriarty use the struggle between evolution and creationism in the story? Examine whether or not the characters' positions ring true, and why. What would you say to those who have different beliefs than yours?

7) How does the car accident that kills Traci affect Evelyn? What motivates Evelyn to initially keep Traci's belongings hidden?

8) Discuss the underlying theme throughout the novel of being chosen or not being chosen.

For a complete readers' guide, visit www.hyperionbooks.com

THE CITY OF YOUR FINAL DESTINATION

Author: Peter Cameron

Publisher: Plume Books, 2003

Website: www.penguin.com

Available in:
Paperback, 320 pages. $14.00
(ISBN 0-452-28430-9)

Subject: Relationships/
Culture & World Issues (Fiction)

Summary

Omar Razaghi, a twenty-eight-year-old doctoral student at the University of Kansas, has won a grant to write a biography of Jules Gund, a deceased Latin American writer. There's just one obstacle: Gund's family has not given him authorization. Undeterred, Omar travels to Uruguay, unannounced, to petition the author's three executors in person: Gund's widow, his much younger mistress, and his brother. Omar's arrival sets in motion a series of events that upsets the precarious balance of life at Ochos Rios, the family's crumbling estate. Long-standing relationships undergo seismic shifts and force the time-stuck inhabitants of Ochos Rios to look toward that most dreaded of places: the future.

Recommended by: Ann Pritchard, *USA Today*

"Delightful, unexpected, magical, romantic and fraught with adorable entanglements."

Author Biography

Peter Cameron's work has appeared in *The New Yorker, The Paris Review,* and *Grand Street.* Author of *Andorra, The Half You Don't Know, Leap Year,* and *The Weekend,* he lives in New York City.

Topics to Consider

1) Compare and contrast Omar's decision to travel to Ochos Rios before and after his journey—what's changed about him; what's stayed the same?

2) Discuss the similarities and differences between Caroline and Arden. Is there significance in the fact that the wife and mistress of the same man live under the same roof?

3) What motivates each member of the Gund literary estate to withhold or support as they do? Of the three members of the Gund family, who carries the most weight, in your opinion, in deciding for or against the biography?

4) In considering her actions throughout the entirety of the novel, what is your opinion of Deirdre? Do you think her motives for pushing Omar to go to Uruguay were legitimate? What was the turning point of her relationship with him, which eventually lead to their break-up?

5) At one point in the novel Omar claims that there can never be a truly "Objective" biography, and that "biography is a hoax" (chapter 7). What does he mean by these statements? Do you agree or disagree with his belief?

6) Consider the author's choice of locales for the novel. How does location figure in the story's events? What if Omar had come from a different university? What if the Gund family lived in the U.S.?

7) What role, if any, does symbolism play? Discuss among the group, for example, the role of the gondola, or Omar's fall from the tree, or Caroline's "tower." What deeper meanings could these events or items hold?

8) Should Omar have, in the end, written Jules Gund's biography? What do you think would be some possible outcomes of the novel, of Omar's life and the lives of the Gund group, if he proceeded and did write the biography?

For a complete reading group guide,
visit www.penguin.com

THE DOGS OF BABEL

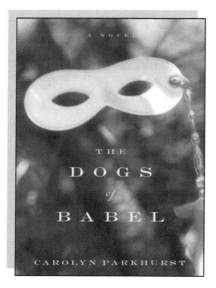

Author: Carolyn Parkhurst

Publisher: Little, Brown
& Company, 2003

Website: www.twbookmark.com

Available in:
Hardcover, 272 pages. $21.95
(ISBN 0-316-16868-8)

Subject: Relationships/
Personal Discovery (Fiction)

Summary

When his wife dies in a fall from a tree in their backyard, linguist Paul Iverson is wild with despair. In the days that follow, Paul becomes certain that Lexy's death was no accident. Strange clues have been left behind: unique, personal messages that only she could have left and that he is determined to decipher. So begins Paul's fantastic and even perilous search for the truth, as he abandons his everyday life to embark on a series of experiments designed to teach his dog Lorelei to communicate. Is this the project of a madman? Or does Lorelei really have something to tell him about the last afternoon of a woman he only thought he knew? At the same time, Paul obsessively recalls the early days of his love for Lexy, and the ups and downs of life with the brilliant, sometimes unsettling woman who became his wife.

Recommended by: *The Boston Globe*

"Elegant and ingenious...An original, charming, and touching novel."

Author Biography

Carolyn Parkhurst holds an MFA in fiction from American University. She lives in Washington, DC, with her husband and their son.

Topics to Consider

1) Paul is a college professor—a man of reason—yet he is determined he can teach his dog Lorelei to talk. What accounts for his strange conviction? Has grief driven him mad, or do his actions have a rational explanation?

2) Paul and Lexy seem to have extremely different personalities. What characteristics in Paul might have drawn Lexy to him? What, for Paul, were the irresistible elements of Lexy's character? Were there early indications that she had a darker side?

3) What do you make of Paul and Lexy's whirlwind romance and courtship? Do they rush into the relationship too quickly, or does the intensity of their feelings for each other indicate a powerful bond?

4) What kind of clues does Paul find to indicate that Lexy's death had more to it than it seemed? Do you think Lexy deliberately left him a puzzle to piece together?

5) How does making death masks affect Lexy? Despite Paul's fears that it is too morbid a pursuit for her, why does she tell Paul she wants to continue?

6) Lexy creates a death mask for a young girl named Jennifer, who committed suicide. Why do Jennifer's parents reject the first mask Lexy makes? What kind of significance does the mask take on for Lexy?

7) Paul's obsession with the Cerberus Society leads him and Lorelei into a dangerous situation. Why is he so fascinated with this strange group? Is he responsible for Lorelei's abduction?

8) Lexy faithfully records her dreams in a dream journal. After her death, Paul hunts through this book searching desperately for answers. What role do dreams play in the book? Do you think they offer a window into a person's psyche? How do Paul's dreams about Lexy reflect how his own grieving process progresses?

9) What is the significance of the verses from Tam Lin that Lexy teaches Paul on pp. 60-61? How does their meaning transform throughout the novel?

THE FIVE PEOPLE YOU MEET IN HEAVEN

Author: Mitch Albom

Publisher: Hyperion, 2003

Website: www.hyperionbooks.com

Available in:
Hardcover, 208 pages. $19.95
(ISBN 0-7868-6871-6)

Subject: Identity/
Personal Discovery (Fiction)

Summary

Eddie is a wounded war veteran, an old man who has lived, in his mind, an uninspired life. His job is fixing rides at a seaside amusement park. On his 83rd birthday, a tragic accident kills him as he tries to save a little girl from a falling cart. He awakes in the afterlife, where he learns that heaven is not a destination. It's a place where your life is explained to you by five people, some of whom you knew, others who may have been strangers. One by one, from childhood to soldier to old age, Eddie's five people revisit their connections to him on earth, illuminating the mysteries of his "meaningless" life, and revealing the haunting secret behind the eternal question: "Why was I here?"

Author Biography

Mitch Albom is the author of the #1 international bestseller *Tuesdays with Morrie.* A nationally syndicated columnist for the *Detroit Free Press* and host of a nationally syndicated program for ABC radio, Albom appears regularly on ESPN and has also been named the top sports columnist in the nation 13 times by the Associated Press Sports Editors of America—the highest honor in his field. He is the founder of The Dream Fund, a charity which helps underprivileged youth study art, and of A Time to Help, a volunteer program. Albom serves on the boards of numerous charities. He lives in Michigan with his wife, Janine. Visit **www.AlbomFivePeople.com**.

Topics to Consider

1) What does Albom mean by saying "All endings are also beginnings?" Share something in your life that has begun as another thing ended, and the events that followed.

2) What does Eddie look like? What kind of guy is he? Look at and discuss some of the details and descriptions that paint a picture of Eddie and his place of business. What is it about an amusement park that makes it a good backdrop for this story?

3) How did counting down the final minutes of Eddie's life affect you?

4) What is the significance of Eddie finding himself in the amusement park again after he dies? What is your reaction when Eddie realizes he's spent his entire life trying to get away from Ruby Pier and he is back there immediately after death? Do you think this is important? Why?

5) Describe what Albom's heaven is like. If it differs from what you imagined, share those differences.

6) Even though Eddie hasn't been reincarnated, consider karma in Eddie's life (where actions would affect his reincarnation). If it isn't karma, what is Albom telling us about life and death?

7) Discuss what you might say to Eddie when he laments that he accomplished nothing with his life or when he asks, "Why would heaven make you relive your own decay?"

8) Examine how Eddie's father's choices and decisions actually shape Eddie's life. Share your own experience of a decision your parents made that affected your life, for better or for worse.

9) Briefly recall the five lessons Eddie learns. How might these be important for all of us? Share which five people might meet you in heaven, and what additional or different lessons might be important to your life. How has this story provided a different perspective of your life?

For a complete readers' guide, visit www.hyperionbooks.com

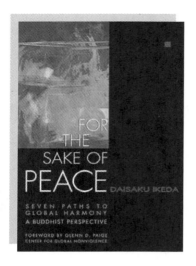

FOR THE SAKE OF PEACE
Seven Paths to Global Harmony

Author: Daisaku Ikeda

Publisher: Middleway Press, 2002

Website: www.middlewaypress.org

Available in:
Paperback, 252 pages. $14.00
(ISBN 0-9674697-9-1)

Subject: Social Issues (Nonfiction)

Summary

The lives of people everywhere were touched by the events in the United States on September 11. Although war, hate, hunger, and terrorism are hardly new to the world, there has been a renewed interest in what it might take to achieve peace across the globe. If you've ever wondered how such a lofty goal could be attained, and how one can make a difference, this book, winner of NAPRA's Nautilus Award in the Social Change category, offers insights, information and wisdom to give readers hope that things can be better.

Drawn from the author's 25+ years of university work and involvement with the United Nations, *For the Sake of Peace* addresses the issue of peace from the perspectives of compassion, the interconnectedness of all life and the absolute respect for human life—principles of Buddhist thought. With an understanding of the mistakes of the past, a clear picture of the emotions and issues that have evolved, and a compassionate message about the possibilities for the future, Dr. Ikeda offers us seven paths to peace—from self-mastery and dialogue to global awareness and disarmament—that will help us overcome major obstacles to the well-being of people everywhere.

Author Biography

Daisaku Ikeda is the founder of numerous cultural and educational institutes throughout the world. He has written more than 200 books that have been translated into several languages, and has worked tirelessly for international cultural exchange and the establishment of world peace.

Topics to Consider

1) Have people you've known experienced war first-hand? Were they able to share what they experienced? Although difficult for most to tell and to hear, discuss the importance of those stories to a society.

2) Since the end of the Cold War in 1989, a time when many felt hopeful for the future, more than fifty nations have been in violent conflicts and millions of lives have been claimed. What were your thoughts about the prospects for world peace at that time? Did they change after September 11? Have those thoughts changed after reading this book?

3) Dialogue is one of the critical steps toward peace, according to Dr. Ikeda. Is there ever a case where dialogue should be halted as a peace-keeping strategy?

4) How might your upbringing have influenced the kind of dialogue with which you feel most comfortable—or, most threatened?

5) Do you agree with the theory that "a borderless economy results in homogenization and a standardized consumer culture?" (p. 78) Is it possible for countries to open their borders to corporations with a global "brand" and still retain their identity? Discuss what you've observed about the strength of cultural identity during your travels to different countries.

6) If, as the author suggests, "the United States represents global society in miniature and foreshadows, for better or worse, the humanity of tomorrow (p. 80)," what changes in the U.S. can help the world achieve harmony?

7) Dr. Ikeda stresses that "We must resist the temptation to assign good exclusively to one side and evil to the other." (p. 115) What role does the news media play in polarizing issues—and people?

8) Many suggest that politicians create war and that if it were up to the people, we would avoid violent conflicts. What evidence supports this belief? What evidence disputes it? What is your personal belief?

GIRL WITH A PEARL EARRING

Author: Tracy Chevalier

Publisher: Plume Books, 2001

Website: www.penguin.com

Available in:
Paperback, 240 pages. $14.00
(ISBN 0-452-28215-2)

Subject: History/Women's Studies/
Coming of Age (Fiction)

Summary

Tracy Chevalier transports readers to a bygone time and place in this richly imagined portrait of the young woman who inspired one of Vermeer's most celebrated paintings. History and fiction merge seamlessly in this luminous novel about artistic vision and sensual awakening. *Girl With a Pearl Earring* tells the story of sixteen-year-old Griet, whose life is transformed by her brief encounter with genius...even as she herself is immortalized in canvas and oil.

Recommended by: *Time* Magazine

"A portrait of radiance... Chevalier brings the real artist Vermeer and fictional muse to life.... A jewel of a novel."

Author Biography

Tracy Chevalier holds a graduate degree in creative writing from the University of East Anglia. An American originally from Washington, D.C., Ms. Chevalier currently lives in London with her husband and son. Visit **www.tchevalier.com.**

Topics to Consider

1) Do you think Griet was typical of other girls her age? In what ways? How did she differ? Did you find her compassionate or selfish? Giving or judgmental?

2) In many ways, the primary relationship in this novel appears to be between Griet and Vermeer. Do you think this is true? How do you feel about Vermeer's relationship with his wife? How does that come into play?

3) Peering into seventeenth century Delft shows a small, self-sufficient city. Where do you think the many-pointed star at the city's center pointed toward? What was happening elsewhere at that time?

4) Discuss the ways religion affected Griet's relationship with Vermeer. His wife? Maria Thins?

5) Maria Thins obviously understood Vermeer's art more than his wife did. Why do you think this was the case? Do you think she shared Griet's talents?

6) Do you think Griet made the right choice when she married the butcher's son? Did she have other options?

7) How is Delft different to or similar to your town or city? Are the social structures comparable?

8) Though *Girl with a Pearl Earring* appears to be about one man and woman, there are several relationships at work. Which is the most difficult relationship? Which is the most promising?

For additional discussion topics, visit www.penguin.com

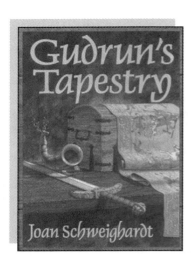

GUDRUN'S TAPESTRY

Author: Joan Schweighardt

Publisher: Beagle Bay Books, 2003

Website: www.beaglebay.com

Available in:
Hardcover, 271 pages. $24.95
(ISBN 0-9679591-3-6)

Subject: History/
Personal Triumph (Fiction)

Summary

Fifth Century Europe holds no greater terror than Attila the Hun—and Gudrun comes to the conclusion that she must be the one to bring him down. Armed only with the cursed sword that was her husband's bane and glory, she sets out alone to avenge her people, the Burgundians. Imprisoned, then enslaved, she reflects back on: the massacre of her people; her love for her husband, the dragon-slayer Sigurd; and his destruction, which brought on her own madness. Now, forced to serve Attila, she schemes with her chief captor, Edeco, Attila's right hand man—a fellow Burgundian who wishes to be her lover. Grounded in history and loosely based on the *Poetic Eddas*, *Gudrun's Tapestry* takes the reader on a quest of self-discovery in a tale of magic and courage that resonates through the centuries to touch the reader's heart and soul.

Recommended by: Diana Paxson, co-author, *Priestess of Avalon*

"...one of the greatest [Germanic] legends from a woman's perspective, with emotion as well as action, bringing new meaning to an ancient tale."

Author Biography

Joan Schweighardt is the author of three critically acclaimed novels. She first conceived of *Gudrun's Tapestry* after studying the Nordic mythology contained in the *Poetic Eddas* while in graduate school at SUNY, then tabled it to work on other projects. She works as a freelance publicist, and continues to write. Joan lives with her husband, son and patient dog in Upstate New York.

Topics to Consider

1) Clearly in the past people had more of a feeling of being "obligated" to their families and extended families. Are we better off now that we don't feel these obligations so intensely? Does it free us up to create our own missions, or does it result in selfishness as a society?

2) Attila the Hun was—undeniably—a beast. Many people died because of him. Was Gudrun right to want to kill him? Or was Sagaria's approach the better choice? How does this tie in to leaders today whom we pretty much all agree are beasts? Should they be assassinated?

3) What was the most difficult part of Gudrun's imprisonment? What would be most difficult for you? Fear? Boredom? Loneliness?

4) Was it the gold or the celebrity (of being a dragon slayer) that motivated Sigurd?

5) Did you feel any sympathy for Brunhild, who apparently grew up in the forest alone and who was madly in love with Sigurd? Did her lack of love growing up and lack of guidance give her license to behave as badly as she does in *Gudrun's Tapestry*? If so, what implications does it have for some of the stories we hear too often today about kids committing crimes?

6) Were you able to forgive Sigurd, as Gudrun did, when he explained how he came to think he was in love with Brunhild? What would you have done?

7) How do you feel about Edeco and his divided loyalties? Were you able to like him in spite of the abusive way he often treated Gudrun? Would you have preferred the book to end with him going off with Gudrun?

8) How did Gudrun's leaving her child make you feel? Could you have done that? Do you think her mission was worth such a sacrifice?

NOTE: The author will be happy to participate in group discussions via speaker phone or e-mail. Contact Jacqueline Simonds at 775/827-8654; 775/827-8633 (fax) or info@beaglebay.com for scheduling. For more about the book, visit:
www.gudrunstapestry.com

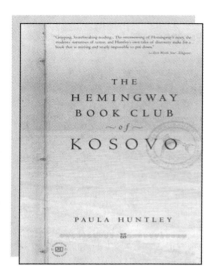

THE HEMINGWAY BOOK CLUB OF KOSOVO

Author: Paula Huntley

Publisher: Tarcher/Putnam, 2003

Website: www.penguinputnam.com

Available in:
Paperback, 236 pages. $13.95
(ISBN 1-58542-293-2)

Subject: Memoir/Culture &
World Issues (Nonfiction)

Summary

Kosovo, 2000. After a decade of brutal civil war and apartheid, volunteers had arrived from all over the world to help. When her husband signed on to help rebuild Kosovo's legal system, Paula Huntley agreed to accompany him for a year. Wanting to make herself useful in some way, Huntley found a job teaching English to a group of Kosovo Albanians in the city of Prishtina. Then, one day, she found an English-language copy of Hemingway's *The Old Man and the Sea* in a bookstore, and an American-style book club was born. This is the diary of Huntley's book club and her other unforgettable experiences in Kosovo.

Recommended by: Mary Pipher, author of *Reviving Ophelia*

"Huntley is an excellent storyteller. This book is filled with heart and intelligence, which is my definition of wisdom."

Author Biography

Paula Huntley was reluctant to give up the familiarity of her life in Northern California, but did so to support her husband Ed's desire to somehow make a difference in Kosovo. Having at one time taught history, she took a course in Teaching English as a Second Language, and brought her personal experience with a book group to her new students.

> If you would like to learn about ways to help young Kosovars receive a good education or about other ways to help the people of Kosovo, please e-mail the author directly at **bookclubofkosovo@yahoo.com**.

Topics to Consider

1) Huntley tries to teach her students about the perils of stereotyping to avoid saying, "All Americans are this, all Serbs are that," and so forth. Do you ever find yourself stereotyping? Why is it so easy or appealing to stereotype?

2) Discuss the notion of collective guilt and collective innocence. Do you feel that the Albanians who unequivocally hate Serbs are justified in their hatred? Do you feel that they can, and should, overcome their hatred for the sake of rebuilding their country?

3) If your country were at war, and someone from the other side burned down your house or killed members of your family, would you be able to overcome your feelings about that person and about his/her people for the sake of moving on?

4) Leonard, the Professor, and Huntley's other students demonstrated incredible hope and optimism despite terrible adversity. What in their lives or in their personalities made this possible? Can you imagine yourself, under the same circumstances, demonstrating such hope and optimism?

5) How can the U.S. and other countries help modernize or democratize Kosovo while respecting their history and differences from other western countries?

6) Do you keep a journal? Can you imagine turning it into a book? When does something that is meaningful to you personally become something that might be meaningful for a wider audience?

7) Have you ever fantasized about dropping everything, seeing the world, and also doing volunteer work in another country? Where do you imagine going? What kind of volunteer work do you imagine doing?

8) Are there lessons we can take from this book—personally, spiritually, politically, and otherwise—that can help us deal with the turmoil of our post-September-11 world?

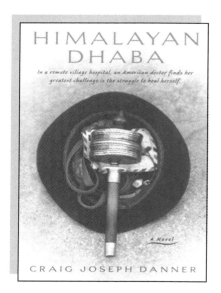

HIMALAYAN DHABA

Author: Craig Joseph Danner

Publisher: Plume Books, 2003

Website: www.penguin.com

Available in:
Paperback, 320 pages. $13.00
(ISBN 0-452-28387-6)

Subject: Personal Triumph/
Culture & World Issues (Fiction)

Summary

After a hair-raising journey, Dr. Mary Davis arrives in a remote Himalayan village with just a backpack and a box of medicines. Expecting to work with a talented Indian surgeon, she finds instead that he is missing and she is now the only doctor for a hundred miles. When an injured tourist stumbles into her overcrowded clinic, he triggers a series of events that connects an unusual mix of characters: Phillip, the spoiled son of a British diplomat; Antone, an aging addict who attempts to kidnap him; Meena, a local village girl who embarks on an improbable rescue; and Amod, the lonely waiter in the *dhaba*, who secretly looks after Mary. Steeped with surprising humor and harrowing detail, *Himalayan Dhaba* reveals a startling variety of human strengths.

Recommended by: *The Salem Evening News*

"An amazing story...Beautifully written and elegantly shaped."

Author Biography

Craig Joseph Danner, a physician's assistant with a degree in creative writing, lives with his wife on a farm in Oregon, where he is at work on his next novel, *The Fires of Edgarville*.

Topics to Consider

1) Does gender play an important role in Mary's journey in this novel? How would the story have been different if Mary had been a man? If Phillip had been a woman?

2) Descent and redemption are major themes of *Himalayan Dhaba*. How do the main characters' paths differ? What does redemption look like to Mary, Amod, Meena and Phillip?

3) At the end of the novel, Phillip stands with his hand out to Mary, announcing his recovery. How do you imagine his long winter with the holy baba has changed Phillip?

4) Ravens appear throughout the novel. What, if anything, do they symbolize?

5) What was your impression of the physical setting of *Himalayan Dhaba*? Do you imagine it to be a beautiful or an ugly place? Would you want to visit this area?

6) Communication—and miscommunication—is another major theme of this novel. How is it that these characters could so dramatically affect each others' lives, even when they could barely communicate with each other verbally?

7) The author leaves the reader to imagine his or her ending to Antone's story. What do you think happens to him next?

8) Violence shapes the lives of both Meena and Manu, yet both of them respond with more violence. Are their responses justifiable? Did you see alternative solutions for either of them?

9) Physical hunger is a recurrent theme in this novel. What does food mean to Amod? To Mary? To Meena? What is food to people of the West that it is not to the indigenous people of this novel and vice versa?

10) Discuss the ways in which religion and faith are addressed in *Himalayan Dhaba*. Some characters are motivated by Christianity, others by Hinduism. Are there characters in the novel to whom spirituality seems absent?

For more information, visit www.himalayandhaba.com.

KLEOPATRA

Author: Karen Essex

Publisher: Warner Books, 2001

Website: www.twbookmark.com

Available in:
Paperback, 385 pages. $13.95
(ISBN 0-446-67917-8)

Subject: History/
Biography (Fiction)

Summary

The cherished daughter of an Egyptian pharaoh, she fought the resentments of a subjugated people and the treachery of her own siblings. Defending her throne from hostile forces on every side, she endured exile, found love, and raised a mercenary army against her enemies...all before she was twenty years old. She was Kleopatra. And this is her untold story. Sweeping from the exotic intrigue of ancient Alexandria to the chaos and corruption of Rome, this novel about one of the most powerful and alluring leaders of all time combines years of exhaustive research with storytelling rich in drama and excitement.

Recommended by: Bruce Feiler, author of *Abraham: A Journey into the Heart of Three Faiths* and *Walking the Bible*

"Mesmerizing...irresistibly sexy. Kleopatra is alluring, cunning, spicy, and alive in a way that is fresh and unforgettable."

Author Biography

Karen Essex is an award-winning journalist, a screenwriter, and the co-author of a biography about cult icon Bettie Page. Born in New Orleans, she holds an MFA in Writing from Goddard College in Vermont. She has recently adapted the Anne Rice novel, *The Mummy, or Ramses the Damned*, into a screenplay for *Titanic* director James Cameron. She has also adapted *Kleopatra* and its sequel, *Pharaoh*, into a screenplay for Warner Bros. She lives in Los Angeles and can be reached at **www.karenessex.com**.

Topics to Consider

1) Why is it that there are no women of today with Kleopatra's great power? Though we are now in post-feminist times, what women of today, if any, have anywhere near her power and influence? What has changed in 2000 years, and what has not?

2) The Romans designed and perpetrated an image of Kleopatra as a sexually wanton overly-ambitious woman. Do we still see women being sexualized in order to be discredited? Do we still see examples that ambition in a woman is a crime, whereas in a man, it is a virtue?

3) Kleopatra used her appearance and style to assert her authority and to speak to her people in symbolic language. Do you see similarities to today's women such as Madonna or Britney Spears?

4) Too many women's stories are told through the stories of the men with whom they were involved. Why is this so, and how would our perception of women be changed if women's stories were told from women's points of view?

5) In Kleopatra's day, the link between religion and government was indelible. Compare the link between religion and government then and now, and how that battle is still being played out in different countries.

6) Imagine if our leaders did not speak English, but communicated to us through interpreters...if only a tiny educated elite spoke the same language as our government officials. How important was it that Kleopatra was the first of her dynasty to speak the language of the people? What does this say about her?

7) The idea of warrior women and warrior queens is not myth but reality. How do the portraits of women like Mohama and Berenike differ from your idea of women of the ancient world?

8) How does this portrait of Kleopatra differ from your impression of her before you read the book?

Visit www.karenessex.com
for additional topics or information about the second book
in this series, **Pharaoh,** *now available in hardcover.*

LAST CALL

Author: Laura Pedersen

Publisher: Ballantine (01/04)

Website:
www.ballantinebooks.com/BRC

Available in:
Paperback, 304 pages. $13.95
(ISBN 0-345-46191-6)

Subject: Humorous Touch/
Faith/Relationships (Fiction)

Summary

Having descended from a long line of indomitable, good-humored Scots, Hayden MacBride sees no reason to take his own death lying down. In fact, he now spends his days crashing funerals for the free food and insight into the Great Beyond. Then he meets Rosamond, a nun playing hooky from the Holy Orders. Hayden is smitten the instant her heavy silver cross smacks him in the face when she leaps up to do the wave at a ball game. Luckily, Rosamond has picked the right person to teach her how to live...and to love—because nobody does both better than Hayden MacBride. But Rosamond's years in the convent have not prepared her for the odd characters of Hayden's world, and his final call at the riotous watering hole called life.

Recommended by: Lorna Landvik, author

"This book will make you laugh and cry and like a good friend, you'll be happy to have made its acquaintance."

Author Biography

Laura Pedersen was born in Buffalo, New York, (one of "God's frozen people") in 1965, at the height of The Folk Music Scare. (For details of misspent youth see essay at **www.literal-latte.com/ pedersen.html**). She started working as the youngest columnist at *The New York Times* and continued writing for the newspaper for the better part of the 1990s. Her first novel, *Going Away Party*, won the Three Oaks Prize for Fiction. Her second, *Beginner's Luck*, has been optioned as a feature film. Laura lives in New York City.

Topics to Consider

1) Have circumstances driven Diana to become more overprotective and fretful than she might be if life were easier—if she had more money and a nice husband, and if her father wasn't ill? Have you ever gone through a rough period when you felt on the verge of a breakdown due to events beyond your control—when life temporarily eclipses your true personality, or at least the person you want to be?

2) Is Hayden a good or bad influence on his grandson? Is Hayden helpful in counteracting Diana's coddling of her son, especially now that he's almost a teenager? Or is Hayden the one making Diana anxious in the first place?

3) Does Hayden's appreciation of the freedom and opportunity he's found in the U.S. combined with fierce pride for his homeland bring to mind mixed attitudes shared by immigrants you know?

4) Does it matter what religion Joey becomes when he's older? Or have Hayden and Rosamond imparted more valuable lessons?

5) Do you know people who have fallen out over religion, or decided not to marry because of the issue? Would you agree or disagree that there are certain situations where the differences and difficulties just can't be overcome?

6) Has Rosamond truly lost her faith, or, as a woman coming to the end of her childbearing years, is she suffering from a vacuum of human affection? Is it possible to live a rich and full life and not know physical intimacy?

7) Being a good parent often involves making difficult choices and personal sacrifices. Give some real-life examples from people you know.

8) By the end of the story has Rosamond converted Hayden or vice versa? Or are they both able to love in their own way and stay true to opposing belief systems?

9) Is it possible to overcome some religious differences by focusing on the similarities?

LITTLE BITTY LIES

Author: Mary Kay Andrews

Publisher: HarperCollins

Website: www.harpercollins.com

Available in:
Hardcover, 448 pages. $24.95
(ISBN 0-06-019959-8)

Subject: Family/
Humorous Touch (Fiction)

Summary

Mary Bliss McGowan doesn't realize her marriage is in trouble until the night she finds a note from her husband Parker telling her he's gone—and taken all the family finances with him. A shocked Mary Bliss had thought everything was just peachy. Of course, there have been so many divorces on her block that the neighborhood is nick-named Split City, and now she's just one of the crowd. But there's nothing usual about the way Mary Bliss handles this dilemma. With an expensive teenaged daughter, a ga-ga mother-in-law in the local nurs-ing home, a big mortgage, and no dough, there's only one thing for her to do: she stages Parker's death and puts in a claim for the insur-ance money.

Recommended by: Anne Rivers Siddons, author of _Low Country_

"Every woman who reads this feast of a book will know her. Every man who reads it will find out what we're really like. What a good book!"

Author Biography

Mary Kay Andrews is a former journalist for the _Atlanta Journal-Constitution_ and has the goods on Atlanta's small neighborhoods.

Topics to Consider

1) Mary Bliss and Katherine have been friends for more than a decade, and the saying "opposites attract" seems to describe their friendship. Are Katharine and Mary Bliss really as different as they seem? What makes their friendship so strong? What do they have in common?

2) Mary Bliss encourages Katherine to reconcile with Charlie, who cheated on Katharine and was living with another woman. Why does she think Katharine should take Charlie back when she makes it very clear that she will not give Parker a second chance?

3) Did Mary Bliss miss any signs that her marriage was not as perfect as she thought? When she finally has the chance to confront Parker, he puts the blame on her for his leaving. What do you think about this?

4) Parker's leaving is the catalyst Mary Bliss needs to make changes in her life—and to change herself. Describe Mary Bliss as she appears at the beginning of the novel. How has she changed by the end of the story?

5) Mary Bliss visits Eula regularly at the nursing home, cooks her favorite foods, and brings her flowers. Even after Parker leaves, Mary Bliss continues to visit Eula. Why is Eula so hostile to Mary Bliss? Why does Mary Bliss feel such a sense of responsibility for Eula? Did Eula's decision about her estate surprise you?

6) Discuss the relationships Mary Bliss has with the women in her life—Katharine, Erin, Eula—and how each one is important to her.

7) Katharine plays an integral role in the plan to fake Parker's death. Why does she do this? Is it merely because she's Mary Bliss's best friend, or are there other reasons?

8) The title of this book, *Little Bitty Lies*, is an understatement. Is there any character who does not resort to lies and deception? In Mary Bliss's case do you feel the ends justified the means?

LONG DAY'S JOURNEY INTO NIGHT

Author: Eugene O'Neill

Publisher: Yale University Press, 2002

Website: www.yalebooks.com

Available in:
Paperback, 180 pages, $12.95
(ISBN 0-300-09305-5)

Subject: Family/
Relationships (Fiction)

Summary

Eugene O'Neill's autobiographical play is regarded as his finest work. First published in 1956, it won the Pulitzer Prize in 1957 and has since sold more than one million copies. This edition includes a new foreword by Harold Bloom, who writes: "The helplessness of family love to sustain, let alone heal, the wounds of marriage, of parenthood, and of sonship, have never been so remorselessly and so pathetically portrayed, and with a force of gesture too painful ever to be forgotten by any of us."

Recommended by: José Quintero

"Only an artist of O'Neill's extraordinary skill and perception can draw the curtain on the secrets of his own family to make you peer into your own. [This play] is the most remarkable achievement of one of the world's greatest dramatists."

Author Biography

Eugene O'Neill (1888-1953), the father of American drama, began writing plays in 1913, and by 1916 his one-act play *Bound East for Cardiff* was produced in New York. In 1920 his full-length play *Beyond the Horizon* was produced and won O'Neill the first of his four Pulitzer Prizes. Over the next few decades, O'Neill published 24 other full-length plays. After receiving the Nobel Prize for literature in 1936, he published two of his most highly acclaimed plays, *The Iceman Cometh* and *A Moon for the Misbegotten*. *Long Day's Journey Into Night* was published three years after his death.

Topics to Consider

1) Discuss O'Neill's use of stage directions. How does the language employed by O'Neill in his directions differ from that spoken by the characters? How do these directions serve to deepen our understanding of action and characters?

2) How does O'Neill conceive of the possibilities of American life? Marriage? Parenthood?

3) How do dreams function to deepen our understanding of the characters? Are any of the characters' dreams attained or attainable?

4) Discuss the issue of substance abuse in the play. What role does it play in the lives of parents and children?

5) Consider the topic of lying. Who lies to whom, when, and for what reasons? Is anyone honest in the play? When?

6) Discuss the subject of monotony—in what the characters do and say, and in the play's setting.

7) Consider the topic of fathers and sons. What kind of relationship does Tyrone have with his two sons? What is the source of the conflict between generations?

LYDIA CASSATT READING THE MORNING PAPER

Author: Harriet Scott Chessman

Publisher: Plume Books, 2002

Website: www.penguin.com

Available in:
Paperback, 176 pages. $13.00
(ISBN 0-452-28350-7)

Subject: History/Women's Studies/
Biography (Fiction)

Summary

Nineteenth-century Paris comes radiantly alive in this richly imagined novel about the intimate relationship between celebrated Impressionist painter Mary Cassatt and her sister, Lydia, Cassatt's fragile, beloved muse. Told in the voice of forty-one-year-old Lydia, this novel opens a window onto a burgeoning world of art and ideas as it captures the extraordinary age in which these sisters lived. This sweeping narrative features real-life figures like Pierre-Auguste Renoir and Edgar Degas, Cassatt's mercurial, charismatic mentor, and includes five full-color plates of Cassatt's paintings. It is a graceful and enchanting exploration of the duels between art and desire, memory and identity, and romantic and familial love.

Recommended by: Alan Cheuse, NPR's *All Things Considered*

"This flowing and lyrical novel...captures a bit of Paris of the time, gives us a teasing portrait of Degas, and brings to the foreground such questions as the relationship of the observer and the observed, and the question of art and morality."

Author Biography

Harriet Scott Chessman has taught modern literature and writing at Yale University. She has published a novel, *Ohio Angels*, essays on art and literature, two children's stories, and an interpretation of Gertrude Stein's writings. She lives with her family in the San Francisco Bay Area.

Topics to Consider

1) Does Lydia's illness permeate her every action or does she transcend its physical limitations?

2) Why is Lydia so jealous of Mary's relationship with Edgar Degas?

3) Degas confesses to Lydia, "You show me how to live, if only I could do it as you do." What does he mean by this? What is Lydia's reaction?

4) How does Lydia feel about being the passive sitter as opposed to the active artist?

5) Lydia tells us that she cherishes her time with Mary, yet she feels guilt that she is keeping Mary from her work, especially when her sister spends time nursing her during intense bouts of her illness. How does this dynamic play out in the story? Does Mary resent having to care for Lydia?

6) How would you describe Lydia's relationship with her mother and father? How does this compare to Mary's relationship with them?

7) What is the message Lydia receives from Mary through her painting, *Driving*? Is this Mary's lasting gift to her dying sister?

8) Because of Lydia's illness, images of mortality—some graphic, others allusive and allegorical—are found throughout the novel. What is the author trying to say about death and life?

9) Lydia says she "can't tell Mary my thoughts, because she can't bear to face illness or death. My whole family's like that." How does Lydia feel about this? What has made her family this way?

For additional discussion topics, visit www.penguin.com

MALCOLM FROM A DISTANCE

Author: Edward H. Garnett

Publisher: Writers Club Press, 2001

Website: www.iuniverse.com

Available in:
Paperback, 243 pages, $14.95
(ISBN 0-595-19842-2)

Subject: Identity/
Social Issues (Fiction)

Summary

Malcolm Merrill is a successful executive at a prestigious advertising firm in Los Angeles. He has a beautiful wife, a gorgeous home, expensive cars, and power at his disposal. In short, Malcolm Merrill seems to exemplify the American dream. So what could possibly possess someone who has it all to attempt suicide? That's the premise of this novel that chronicles the life of a man whose perfect world suddenly crumbles beneath him—a man forced to come to terms with all he sacrificed on his rise to the top: his family, his friends, and his soul.

Recommended by: Dana Brookins, Edgar Allan Poe Award-winning author

"The characterization is powerful and I found myself totally intrigued with the story. Reading this novel turned into something fascinating that, when I had to go away, made me eager to return."

Author Biography

Edward H. Garnett has been involved in screenwriting, fiction, and other forms of writing since 1986. Mr. Garnett's work has been published in magazines such as *Haunts* and *The Write Thing*. His short stories have been accepted for publication in *Thin Ice, Crossroads,* and *The Circle* magazines. In addition, his original screenplay, *The Ties That Bind,* was judged to be within the top 6% of the 3,514 scripts submitted to a Nicholl Fellowships in Screenwriting competition.

Topics to Consider

1) A pattern established early in the novel is that Malcolm places the demands of his job over the needs of his family. What possesses him to act this way? How might he have done things differently?

2) Although Malcolm has seniority and years of work experience on his side, he views newcomer Leonard Bolander as a threat. Why does Malcolm feel this way? Is he being rational?

3) What significance does Malcolm's new car have in the novel? How does his opinion about this vehicle change throughout the book?

4) Malcolm's wife, Joanne, is frustrated by her husband's behavior and she makes a radical choice that forever changes each member of her family. Are her actions justified? Why or why not?

5) The notion of betrayal surfaces at various points in this novel. List some examples of betrayal found in this book. How does each instance directly relate to the protagonist, Malcolm? Why is he afraid to confide in those people who are closest to him?

6) The circumstances in this novel create a downward spiral that established the suicidal tendencies in Malcolm. Do you feel he really wants to kill himself? Support your viewpoint with examples from the novel.

7) Describe Malcolm's relationship with his sons, Jason and Trenton. How do the relationships change in the course of the book?

8) Why is the racquetball game between Malcolm, Carl, Leonard, and Donald so important? What does this game really symbolize?

9) Discuss Malcolm's attraction, and ultimate actions, regarding Betsy. What does Malcolm learn from his "escape" to Lake Tahoe?

10) Should Malcolm reconcile with his oldest son, Trenton, or has too much damage occurred between them to allow these characters to reunite?

11) Does Malcolm resolve his problems by the end of the novel? Do you agree with his decisions?

MARRIAGE: A DUET

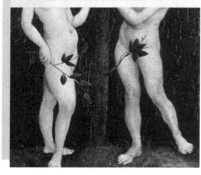

Author: Anne Taylor Fleming

Publisher: Hyperion, 2003

Website: www.hyperionbooks.com

Available in:
Paperback, 192 pages. $12.95
(ISBN 0-7868-8761-3)

Subject: Relationships (Fiction)

Summary

Two novellas offer a unique perspective on infidelity, bringing into sharp focus the complications and consequences created by spouses who—despite their genuine bond of love—are unfaithful to one another. In the first, Caroline, a middle-aged woman, keeps a careful vigil over her husband William's death bed. While frightened by the idea of losing her soulmate and lifelong companion, Caroline confronts another startling reality: she feels a kind of rebirth through his passing.

In the second novella, David—husband, father, and businessman—finds his sense of well-being and achievement damaged by his wife Marcia's betrayal: a one-night affair, which she regrets but does not conceal from him.

Recommended by: *The Baltimore Sun*

"Stellar...intensely believable characters and elegant prose."

Author Biography

Anne Taylor Fleming is a nationally recognized journalist and *CNN NewsNight* contributor. She is a regular on-camera essayist for the *NewsHour with Jim Lehrer* and the author of *Motherhood Deferred: A Woman's Journey.* This is her first work of fiction. Fleming lives in Los Angeles with her husband, journalist Karl Fleming.

Topics to Consider

1) Discuss the first few pages of *A Married Woman*. What are your first impressions of "Mom" (Caroline), Kate and Stevie? What do you learn about William? Who is narrating?

2) What is Caroline's reaction to her husband's affair? What is your opinion about William's affair? For Caroline, why would there be "no scenes, not on her part"? Is she passive, or is something else going on?

3) Articulate what Caroline's feelings are about her life. What would you say to her if you could talk to her?

4) What is Caroline's experience of sex in her marriage? What does it represent? What is William's sexual relationship with Caroline?

5) Look at the hospital scenes and Caroline's observations about the hospital routine. If you've spent much time in one, how do you feel about Fleming's evocation of the hospital experience?

6) Comparing the two stories in *Marriage: A Duet*, what are some of the reasons that David (in *A Man's Marriage*) can reveal his emotions while Caroline (in *A Woman's Marriage*) cannot?

7) Is there any truth to the old stereotype about women being more forgiving and men more possessive? Consider the affairs in both stories and discuss whether or not this idea has merit.

8) Compare and contrast the coping mechanisms to the cheating in both stories in *Marriage: A Duet*, for example, David's use of sarcasm and Caroline's quiet. Which character do you relate to, and why?

9) Looking at *A Married Man*, why do you think that Marcia strays? In *A Married Woman*, why does William stray? Why don't Caroline and David stray? What, if any, were the warning signs that the cheaters were going to cheat? Discuss whether or not these stories depict what actually happens when infidelity occurs, and why fiction can be a good device for exposing this common and very painful occurrence.

For a complete readers' guide, visit www.hyperionbooks.com

MINIATURES

Author: Norah Labiner

Publisher: Coffee House Press, 2003

Website:
www.coffeehousepress.org

Available in:
Paperback, 381 pages. $16.00
(ISBN 1-56689-151-5)

Subject: Intrigue/
Relationships (Fiction)

Summary

A scandalous literary suicide, two decades of hushed intrigue, and a bundle of controversial letters fuel this novel, as told by Fern Jacobi, a young American who stumbles into the mystery on her travels through Ireland. She meets up with the renowned author Owen Lieb, who has just returned to Galway with his second wife after years of self-imposed exile. The couple befriends Fern, who comes to work for them cleaning their long abandoned home. As the days of autumn turn short and dark, Fern begins to unravel the whole truth behind the speculation surrounding Owen's first wife, who killed herself at the age of 30 and has since become a cult icon. *Miniatures* is a story of obsession and celebrity, fog and shadows, and the ordinary mysteries that haunt even the most extraordinary love affairs.

Recommended by: *Kirkus Reviews*

"A splendid, leisurely meditation on the meaning of fame, identity, and love that reaches real depths of thought and feeling."

Author Biography

Norah Labiner's debut novel, *Our Sometime Sister,* was a finalist for the Barnes & Noble *Discover Great New Writers* Award. Labiner was named as one of the ten "novelists who are changing the way we see the world" by *Utne* magazine. She is a 2002 National Endowment for the Arts Fellow and lives in Minneapolis.

Topics to Consider

1) The setting is very important to *Miniatures*. What is added to the story by placing the action in Ireland? What role does the grand, brooding house play? Does it bring to mind other houses from literature?

2) Describe the effect of Fern's narrative voice on the tone and emotional impact of the book. How would the book be different if Labiner had chosen a totally objective narrator? A third person point of view? Does the fact that Fern becomes so intimately involved in her narrative lead up to the surprise ending?

3) The lives of Owen and Franny Lieb resemble the lives of poets Ted Hughes and Sylvia Plath. In what ways are the fictional and factual stories similar/different? Knowing this historical element, discuss the significance of Fern's fascination with celebrity biographies. How is this fascination reflected in American culture?

4) While telling the Liebs' story, Fern reflects on her relationships with Newton Graves and Alexander Piltdown. Do her relationships with these men parallel the relationships between Owen and Franny? Esther? Brigid? In what way does observing the Liebs affect Fern's feelings toward these men?

5) Labiner explores ethnic tensions between Owen's Jewish heritage and his wives' German background. How does this affect Owen's relationships with his wives? Do Franny and Brigid react differently/similarly to the tension?

6) Keeping in mind Fern's statements about truthful and glamorized biographies, discuss whether she is a trustworthy biographer/ autobiographer or not. Does she either consciously or unconsciously color the truth of what happened?

7) At the end of the book Fern writes, "A good way for a story to end is with someone dying and someone else valiantly carrying on. I don't think this is how my story will end." What will happen to Fern once she finishes her manuscript? How will her story end?

THE MIRACLES OF SANTO FICO

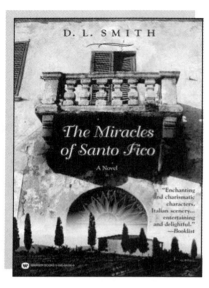

Author: D.L. Smith

Publisher: Warner Books, 2003

Website: www.twbookmark.com

Available in:
Paperback, 368 pages. $13.95
(ISBN 0-446-69036-8)

Subject: Personal Discovery
(Fiction)

Summary

When Leo Pizzola returns from America to Santo Fico—a tiny, forgotten village in Tuscany—he discovers more than the now neglected vineyard of his childhood. There's Marta, Leo's first and only true love, who will barely speak to him now; Topo, his once trusting, but now leery, best friend; and Father Elio, the village's pillar of faith who is experiencing a spiritual crisis all his own. When Leo and Topo are forced to orchestrate a series of manmade miracles—each more botched than the last—the end results are truly...miraculous. *The Miracles of Santo Fico* pours forth with the stories of a village that is rediscovering the beauty of life itself and the nature and meaning of miracles.

Recommended by: *Kirkus Reviews* (starred review)

"A delightful fable, told with wit and grace."

Author Biography

D.L. Smith lives in Oregon with his wife and two sons.

Topics to Consider

1) Which of the events in this book would you truly consider a miracle? Do true miracles occur without human intervention—or because of it? List each of the events that might be considered miraculous, and decide a) if the event actually occurred or it was a figment of the villagers'—or readers'—imagination and b) which of the miracles was most important in saving the village.

2) Regret and forgiveness are two of the main themes running throughout the novel. Is there a central character who has no regrets? Which character does the best job of rectifying his or her regrets? Why? Do the characters tend to have more trouble forgiving themselves than others?

3) Does Father Elio's secret undercut his ability to heal his village? His power as a priest? Do you think he was right or wrong to have held on to his secret for so long? If you lived in the village, what would be your reaction to this secret?

4) Marta is clearly a woman who has had difficulty with love. Who do you think she actually loved more, Franco or Leo? What do you imagine would have happened had Leo not left that fateful day? Is Marta justified in her antipathy toward Leo? Can you pinpoint the moment when her feelings start to turn?

5) When Leo and Topo set out to orchestrate miracles, do you think they were justified in tampering with the lives of their fellow townspeople? Are any of the characters worse off for their efforts?

6) Marta and Carmen are a wonderful example of the troubles mothers and daughters can go through. Should Marta have granted Carmen more leverage in making her own mistakes, or was she obliged to stop history from repeating itself? Can you think of a parallel in your family life? How did/would you handle it?

7) Was Leo justified in orchestrating Carmen's attack on the beach, considering the danger he put her in? What else might he have done to bring Carmen and Paolo together and eliminate Solly in one stroke?

8) Santo Fico started out a sleepy little village, plagued by a collective loss of faith. How would you describe the village at the book's end? Try to imagine each character's future. Can you predict where each of the central characters will be in five years?

NOT FADE AWAY
A Short Life Well Lived

**Author: Laurence Shames &
Peter Barton**

Publisher: Rodale, 2003

Website: www.rodale.com

Available in:
Hardcover, 224 pages. $22.95
(ISBN 1-57954-688-9)

Subject: Biography/
Personal Challenges (Nonfiction)

Summary

In the prime of Peter Barton's life, happily married and the father of three children, he came face to face with the greatest challenge in a life filled with risk-taking and direction-changing. Diagnosed with cancer, he began a journey that was frightening and appalling, yet also full of wonder and discovery. His journey is re-created in the alternating voices of Peter himself and Laurence Shames; both men are close in age yet have made vastly different choices in life. As friends and co-authors, they relive the high points of years that embody the hopes and strivings of an entire generation and find universal meaning in Peter's confrontation with his own mortality.

Recommended by: Jim Lehrer

"...A little masterpiece...a book to be read by everyone, by anyone of any age who dares to share a special life and death....[It] may be the most honest book I have ever read."

Author Biography

Peter Barton was a founder and CEO of Liberty Media and a passionate advocate for innovative cable programming. After leaving Liberty in 1997, he devoted himself to philanthropy and education; he taught a graduate business course in entrepreneurship and founded the nonprofit Privacy Foundation. He died in September, 2002.

Laurence Shames, formerly the Ethics columnist for *Esquire*, is a critically acclaimed novelist and was the ghostwriter of the *NYT* best-seller *Boss of Bosses*. He lives in Ojai, California.

Topics to Consider

1) How does the death of Peter's father at such a young age influence his life choices? Does it enable him to pursue his own life with such fervor?

2) Peter is described as both an Everyman and an emblem of Baby-Boomer possibility. What has changed since the baby-boomer period that makes such an opportunity more elusive?

3) Do you think Peter's distrust of authority/religion accurately represents his generation? How does the growth of his personal faith affect his ability to face death?

4) Peter calls himself "a lucky man." Do you agree? Would you barter time for the chance and the courage to live as he did?

5) How does the relationship between Peter and Laurence color the narrative? Does Laurence Shames succeed in capturing the spirit of Peter in both life and death?

6) Peter's cancer becomes its own character throughout the book, equipped with needs, goals, and its own agenda. Does his rationalization of the disease aid in his ability to understand and ultimately surrender to it?

7) What aspect of Peter will linger and affect you most?

8) Do you see the production of the book as a selfless or selfish act by Peter? How do you think its existence will help his family and children cope? Can the book be seen as a vehicle allowing his children to know him as a man as they get older?

9) Music remains a constant theme throughout the book and Peter's life. How do you feel the Buddy Holly/Rolling Stones lyric "Love is love and not fade away" helps to tie this all together? Though not quite logical, what feelings does the statement evoke and how does this relate to the way in which Peter saw time at the end of his life?

ON BEING HUMAN
Where Ethics, Medicine and Spirituality Converge

Author: Daisaku Ikeda, René Simard, Guy Bourgeault

Publisher: Middleway Press, 2003

Website: www.middlewaypress.org

Available in:
Paperback, 288 pages. $15.95
(ISBN 0-9723267-1-5)

Subject: Social Issues/
Inspirational/Faith (Nonfiction)

Summary

This exploration of what it means to be healthy from a physical, mental, and spiritual standpoint discusses Western humanism, Japanese Buddhism, and modern science from three divergent, yet expert, perspectives. Seeking common ground through dialogue, this ambitious work broaches questions about issues that face today's society, such as cancer, AIDS, death with dignity, in vitro fertilization, biomedical ethics, and more. The discussions cut through linguistic and cultural barriers to present a vision of the potential and the inherent challenges of being human.

Recommended by: Lou Marinoff, author of *Plato Not Prozac*

"Informative and hopeful, it offers wise perspectives on life and death, revealing their deeper meaning and higher purpose."

Author Biography

Daisaku Ikeda is president of the Soka Gakkai International, one of the most dynamic lay Buddhist associations in the world today. Spiritual leader for millions, he is widely recognized as one of the leading interpreters of Buddhist thought, bringing its timeless wisdom to bear on contemporary issues confronting humanity. Eminent medical scientist **René Simard** was rector of the University of Montreal from 1993 to 1998. Bioethicist **Guy Bourgeault** is Professor of Ethics at the University of Montreal. All have worked to deepen understanding of the relationship between medical science and the ethical concern for the future of individuals, whole societies, and the human race.

Topics to Consider

1) When some companies today are promoting remedies that are untested and not even built upon scientific theory, what constitutes a sensible and balanced approach to health given the deluge of new products and services?

2) What is your own belief about the relationship between physical and psychological health? Which of your beliefs are shaped by science, faith or personal experience?

3) Dr. Simard suggests, "Patients know more about their own physical condition than others think." Do you agree? Discuss the changes in the doctor-patient relationship you've observed over the years as the Internet and other resources have allowed people to learn more about their health issues.

4) Throughout history there have been contagious and deadly diseases. Are there ways to avoid public hysteria when a new disease surfaces? How would you respond personally if you were a medical professional facing an unknown but deadly disease?

5) Do you believe that stress is the spice of life? What were the circumstances of the single most defining experience that shaped your life? Can one's character grow as intensely during good times?

6) After reading the dialogue on bioethics and the complex issues regarding cloning, definitions of life and death, and quality of life, how were your own beliefs affected?

7) Dr. Ikeda states, "The real meaning of youth has nothing to do with physical age." What are your personal views of aging? What significance does age have, if any?

8) Dr. Ikeda suggests that "learning about death enriches life." How might your day-to-day life be influenced by your beliefs about death? How can we "bravely face death instead of ignoring it?"

9) Do you agree that there is a greater need for debate in our culture? Discuss the role of various stakeholders (e.g. the media, educational systems, houses of worship) in the effort to encourage dialogue.

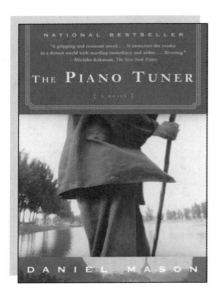

THE PIANO TUNER

Author: Daniel Mason

Publisher: Vintage Books, 2003

Website: www.readinggroupcenter.com

Available in: Paperback, 336 pages. $14.00 (ISBN 1-4000-3038-2)

Subject: History/ Culture & World Issues (Fiction)

Summary

When Edgar Drake is summoned to the British War Office and asked to tune an eccentric major's grand piano in the jungles of Burma, he is both confused and intrigued. The year is 1886, and the British Empire is attempting to tighten its control of its colonies in the Far East, to fend off French rivals in the Mekong Delta, and to quell the resistance of a confederacy of local Shan tribes in northern Burma. Surgeon-Major Anthony Carroll has established an important foothold in Mae Lwin, employing unconventional methods—reciting poetry and playing music—to negotiate treaties with Burmese opponents of British rule. As Edgar embarks on his first trip abroad, the beauty and mystery of Burma, its entrancing landscape, its customs and music, and an exotic woman named Khin Myo cast a spell that he cannot resist.

Recommended by: Michiko Kakutani, *The New York Times*

"A gripping and resonant novel.... It immerses the reader in a distant world with startling immediacy and ardor.... Riveting."

Author Biography

Daniel Mason received his bachelor's degree in biology from Harvard College in 1998, and spent a year researching malaria on the Thai-Myanmar border, where much of *The Piano Tuner* was written. He is currently a medical student at the University of California, at San Francisco. *The Piano Tuner* is his first novel.

Topics to Consider

1) Why does Edgar decide to accept a mission to travel thousands of miles to tune a piano in a remote and dangerous jungle at the furthest outreaches of the British Empire? Why does his wife, Katherine, encourage him to go?

2) As he contemplates his voyage to Burma, Edgar views London on a foggy night: "He could see the vague line of the shore, the vast, heavy architecture that crowded the river. Like animals at a waterhole, he thought, and he liked the comparison" [p. 23]. Why is this a particularly apt simile for Edgar to use at this moment? Where else in the novel does Mason reveal the depth of Edgar's consciousness through his impressions?

3) After he's been away from London for several months, Edgar writes to Katherine that he has changed, although, he admits "What this change means I don't know, just as I don't know if I am happier or sadder than I have ever been" [p. 252]. How has Edgar changed? What has changed him? What is his real purpose in Burma?

4) What kind of woman is Khin Myo? Is her attraction to Edgar real or feigned? What is her relationship to Anthony Carroll? How is she related to the woman with the parasol at the beginning and end of the story?

5) What roles does music play in the novel? How does it affect its listeners? What is its ultimate importance in the story?

6) At the end of the novel, Captain Nash-Burnham tells Edgar that Anthony Carroll is a traitor to England and suggests a number of possible roles for the Doctor: Edgar thinks Carroll is a genius and a peacemaker. Which of these interpretations is correct? Does the novel present enough evidence to decide?

7) What does the novel as a whole suggest about the British Empire—its effects on colonized peoples and on those who try to rule them—in the late nineteenth century? How is this historical portrait relevant to our own time and the political and cultural conflicts between the West and the Middle East?

For a complete Reading Group Guide,
visit www.readinggroupcenter.com

QUEST FOR LIFE

Author: Barbara Rothe Merin

Publisher: Coastal Villages Press, 2003

Website: www.coastal-villages.com

Available in:
Paperback, 272 pages. $14.95
(ISBN 1-882943-17-1)

Subject: Family /Relationships/
Inspiration /Faith (Fiction)

Summary

Andrea and John's blissful marriage of five years shatters with the mysterious death of her son, Billy. Andrea's large blended family suffers over this tragedy and Andrea's deep depression threatens her relationship with John. Andrea's daughter, Lizzie, is obsessed with her role in her brother's death and distances herself from her mother, who searches for solace in many ways. Lizzie flees in her quest for answers to an ancient Buddhist temple in southeast Asia where she meets Han, an attractive Turkish Muslim. Andrea confronts unexpected challenges with John and his family when astonishing events unfold regarding Billy's death. Floundering in the sea of life, can Andrea resolve Billy's loss, and can Lizzie, in her quest for life as a young woman, grasp the rescue ring of her family and will Han?

Recommended by: Ron Rash, author of *One Foot in Eden*

"This is a haunting novel about the search for understanding and redemption in the midst of a family tragedy. Barbara Merin is unafraid to confront what William Faulkner called 'the human heart in conflict with itself.' This story is ripe for group discussion."

Author Biography

Barbara Merin is the author of *Passionate Visions* and *Rescue Ring: We Are All Touched.* Merin's life work with families provides research for her books about family dynamics, including death, grief and bereavement.

Topics to Consider

1) Reviewers say this contemporary story deals with Christian and family values our society yearns for. How do you respond to this claim? What have proven to be the most valuable ways to address values in your own family?

2) How do family members break the cloud cycle of guilt and grief to survive a suicide or an accidental death? Is it ever possible to explain what forces drive people to suicide? Why is this so vitally important to surviving family members?

3) Andrea's search for solace leads her to drink, see a psychiatrist, lean on her husband, John, prayer. Which was *the* most important in her recovery?

4) Lizzie's quest for life takes her to a medium, a psychiatrist, meditation, time in Java with a monk in a monastery, and also to sagacious Aunt Tessa, Han, her epiphany at St. Peter's, her mother's support. Which helped Lizzie *the* most in her quest for life? What helps you?

5) What do you think of John and Andrea's marriage, their blended family relationships? How are the elements of equality, duty, honesty handled in their marriage? How are they dealt with in your marriage, in most marriages?

6) *Quest For Life* probes the complexity of the word "family." What is a "real" family. Andrea's includes a gay daughter, her partner and an adopted Asian granddaughter. Andrea has an illegitimate five-year-old grandson, a daughter in love with a Turkish Muslim, and three young adult stepchildren and their families. What relationships do you have in your "real family?"

7) If your book club wanted to speak with the author regarding this book, or its creation, what would you most want to ask?

For more information, or to contact the author about taking part in your group discussion, please visit www.bmerinbooks.com

THE QUILTER'S APPRENTICE

Author: Jennifer Chiaverini

Publisher: Plume Books, 2000

Website: www.penguin.com

Available in:
Paperback, 271 pages. $13.00
(ISBN 0-452-28172-5)

Subject: Relationships/
Women's Studies (Fiction)

Summary

When Sarah McClure and her husband, Matt, move to Waterford, Pennsylvania, she hopes to make a fresh start in the small college town. Unable to find a job that is both practical and fulfilling, she takes a temporary position at Elm Creek Manor helping its reclusive owner Sylvia Compson prepare her family estate for sale after the death of her estranged sister. Sylvia is also a master quilter and, as part of Sarah's compensation, offers to share the secrets of her creative gifts with the younger woman. During their lessons, the intricate, varied threads of Sylvia's life begin to emerge. As the bond between them deepens, Sarah resolves to help Sylvia free herself from remembered sorrows and restore her life—and her home—to its former glory. In the process, she confronts painful truths about her own family, even as she creates new dreams for the future.

Recommended by: *The Dallas Morning News*

"Jennifer Chiaverini's Elm Creek Quilts series...have become classics of their time."

Author Biography

Jennifer Chiaverini lives with her husband and two sons in Madison, Wisconsin. In addition to the five volumes in the Elm Creek Quilt series, she is the designer of the Elm Creek Quilts line from Red Rooster fabrics. Learn more at **www.elmcreek.net.**

Topics to Consider

1) What is Sarah McClure hoping to find when she moves with her husband Matt to Waterford, PA? Does she really believe that she can make a fresh start in this small college town, or is she just making the best of things? Does she seem happy in her marriage? What do you think she really wants?

2) Why is Sarah so drawn to the quilt she first sees at Elm Creek Manor? What does this luminous, light-filled creation symbolize for her, in terms of love and loss and her earlier life?

3) Sylvia Compson lived through the horror and heartbreak of World War II. How did these experiences change her? What role does quilt-making play in her life today? How has the recent loss of her sister Claudia affected Sylvia? What about a much earlier tragedy?

4) Describe the relationship that develops between Sylvia and Sarah. What does each woman get out of this friendship? In what ways does Sylvia remind Sarah of her own grandmother?

5) Teaching Sarah how to quilt fulfills something very profound in Sylvia. Explain what you think that is, and how it ties in to the major themes of the book.

6) How does Sarah help Sylvia to finally accept her past? How does Sylvia help Sarah come to terms with her past? How do both women help each other prepare for the future?

7) "Sorrows come to us all," Sylvia's great-aunt once said to her. How does the adult Sylvia translate this portentous statement into the creation of dark and light sections of a quilt? If red squares "keep the fires burning," what do the other colors symbolize?

8) What kinds of changes do Sarah and Sylvia undergo by the book's end? What have they discovered about friendship, acceptance, loyalty, and love?

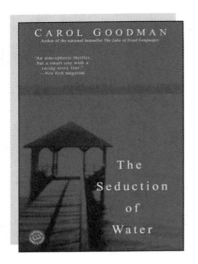

THE SEDUCTION
OF WATER

Author: Carol Goodman

Publisher: Ballantine (01/04)

Website: www.ballantinebooks.com/
BRC

Available in:
Paperback, 384 pages. $13.95
(ISBN 0-345-45091-4)

Subject: Intrigue (Fiction)

Summary

Iris Greenfeder, ABD (All But Dissertation), feels the "buts" are taking over her life: all but published, all but a professor, all but married. Yet the sudden impulse to write a story about her mother, Katherine Morrissey, leads to a shot at literary success. The piece recounts an eerie Irish fairy tale her mother used to tell her at bedtime—and nestled inside it is the sad story of her death. It captures the attention of her mother's former literary agent, who is convinced that Katherine wrote one final manuscript before her strange, untimely end in a fire thirty years ago. So Iris goes back to the remote Hotel Equinox in the Catskills, the place where she grew up, to write her mother's biography and search for the missing manuscript—and there she unravels a haunting mystery, one that holds more secrets than she ever expected.

Recommended by: *New York* magazine

"An atmospheric thriller, but a smart one with a racing story line."

Author Biography

Carol Goodman is the author of *The Lake of Dead Languages*. Her work has appeared in such journals as *The Greensboro Review*, *Literal Latté*, *The Midwest Quarterly*, and *Other Voices*. She taught Latin for several years in Austin, Texas, then received an M.F.A. in fiction from the New School University. Goodman currently teaches writing and works as a writer-in-residence for Teachers & Writers. She lives on Long Island.

Topics to Consider

1) Discuss your favorite fairy tale from your childhood. How did you learn the story and what did you learn from it? What does it mean to you now?

2) Both Iris and Phoebe are haunted by the early loss of their mothers. Discuss how these characters have been shaped by and have adapted to their losses and more generally how the death of a parent or a parental figure affects us all.

3) A schism exists in Iris's life before and after her mother's death. Do you have such a defining event in your life? Discuss the various life-changing events—births, deaths, and other rites of passage—that can result in such a before-and-after outlook.

4) When Iris begins to investigate her mother's past, she comes to understand that her mother felt like an imposter in her new life at the Hotel Equinox. Why is this so? Discuss the many reasons why people might feel like an imposter in their own lives.

5) The financial and personal toll exacted in securing the time and space to create art is central to this novel. Discuss the hurdles that artists face. Do you think female artists still confront more obstacles than their male counterparts?

6) Thinking about her relationship with Jack, Iris speculated, "Lover and beloved. Didn't there always have to be one of each?" Do you agree?

7) The seven-year age difference between Aidan and Iris troubles Iris greatly. Do you think the pairing of older women and younger men—as opposed to the reverse—still carries a social stigma? Is this changing?

8) Do you think learning the full truth about her mother will set Iris free to live her own life on her own terms?

9) What do you think would have happened to Kay and her family if she had told her husband the whole truth about her past? Could the tragedies that followed have been averted?

SUGAR

Author: Bernice L. McFadden

Publisher: Plume Books, 2001

Website: www.penguin.com

Available in:
Paperback, 229 pages. $13.00
(ISBN 0-452-28220-9)

Subject: Social Issues/Relationships/
Women's Studies (Fiction)

Summary

Evoking the rich atmosphere of the deep South, *Sugar* tells the story of a young prostitute who comes to Bigelow, Arkansas, to start a new life. Sugar moves next door to Pearl, who is still grieving for the daughter who was murdered fifteen years before. Over sweet potato pie, an unlikely friendship begins, transforming both their lives—and the life of an entire community. *Sugar* brings a 1950s black town vibrantly to life with its flowering magnolia trees, lingering scents of jasmine and honeysuckle, and white picket fences that keep strangers out—but ignorance and superstition in. To read this novel is to take a journey through loss and suffering to a place of forgiveness, understanding and grace.

Recommended by: *Ebony*

"Sugar *sings with unforgettable images, unique characters, and a moving story line. It's a haunting story that keeps the pages turning until the end.*"

Author Biography

Bernice L. McFadden is the author of the national bestsellers *Loving Donovan, This Bitter Earth,* and *The Warmest December* (shortlisted for the Hurston/Wright Foundation Legacy Award). She lives in Brooklyn, New York, where she is at work on her fifth novel. Visit the author's website at **www.bernicemcfadden.com**.

Topics to Consider

1) *Sugar* opens with the murder of Jude Taylor. Why do you think the author chose to open with this graphic—and horrific—scene? How did this scene set the tone for the rest of the novel? Why is Jude's murder such an integral part of the storyline?

2) By associating with Sugar, Pearl alienates Shirley and some of the other women in Bigelow. Why do these women feel so threatened by Sugar?

3) Sugar and Pearl's friendship is an unlikely pairing. What does each one gain from the relationship?

4) Why do Pearl and Sugar choose to confide in one other when neither has ever done so with anyone else?

5) In the beginning of the book, the author has included this quote by Sarah Miles: "There's a little bit of hooker in every woman. A little bit of hooker and a little bit of God." What do you think of this statement? How does it pertain to the story?

6) *Sugar* is set mainly in the small town of Bigelow, Arkansas. What "role" does the small town play in the story? Sugar was raised in a small town by the Lacey sisters and later lived in St. Louis, Detroit, and Chicago. Why does she choose to return to a small town?

7) Describe Pearl and Joe's relationship. What first drew them to one another? How would you describe their relationship when the story first begins? How does it change as the novel progresses? At the end of the story, the reader finds out that Joe is going to make a confession to Pearl. How do you think she would have reacted to the news?

8) Why does Pearl feel so bereft by Sugar's departure? Do you think she sensed that Sugar was more than just a neighbor and friend to her and Joe?

For additional discussion topics, visit www.penguin.com

THE SUNDAY WIFE

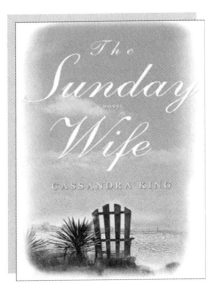

Author: Cassandra King

Publisher: Hyperion, 2003

Website: www.HyperionBooks.com

Available in:
Paperback, 400 pages. $14.00
(ISBN 0-7868-9044-4)

Subject: Personal Discovery/
Identity/Women's Studies (Fiction)

Summary

Married for 20 years to the Reverend Benjamin Lynch, a handsome, ambitious minister of the prestigious Methodist church, Dean Lynch has never quite adjusted her temperament to the demands of the role of a Sunday wife. When her husband is assigned to a larger and more demanding community in the Florida panhandle, Dean becomes fast friends with Augusta Holderfield, a woman whose good looks and extravagant habits immediately entrance her. As their friendship evolves, Augusta challenges Dean to break free from her traditional role as the preacher's wife. Just as Dean is questioning everything she has always valued, a tragedy occurs, providing the catalyst for change in ways she never could have imagined.

Recommended by: Anne Rivers Siddons, author

"A wonderful book. Cassandra King catches these quirky, complex people and their world flawlessly."

Author Biography

Cassandra King was born in Alabama, where she taught college-level English and writing. She now lives in South Carolina with her husband, author Pat Conroy.

Topics to Consider

1) What is a Sunday wife? What makes a "good" one? Consider whether or not Dean fits the bill, and explain your reasoning.

2) What is the role of religion in *The Sunday Wife*? How does it frame—or anchor—the story? Share who you believe holds the book's moral center, and why.

3) Examine why King uses different social issues and dilemmas—like same-sex marriage, psychic healing, book banning and adultery—to tell this story.

4) Were you surprised at Dean's early admission that she and Ben don't share a bedroom? What kind of relationship does this lead you to believe that they have?

5) When Dean succeeds in cultivating a friendship with Augusta and Maddox, why isn't Ben ecstatic? Explore whether or not Augusta causes a rift between Ben and Dean. Is Dean and Ben's relationship already coming apart?

6) How are Dean and Augusta alike? What are your impressions of them? Discuss their similarities and differences between Ben and Maddox, what kind of men you think they are, and why.

7) Dean and Augusta talk about fate vs. determination and choice. Share whether or not you believe, as Augusta does, that there are unseen forces that determine our fate. Why? How do Augusta's beliefs fit with what happens in her life?

8) Explore the turmoil Rich and Godwin's union causes the community. Why is Ben so upset about Rich and Godwin's union? Why was he so unsympathetic about Dean being attacked? What would you say to him if you were Dean?

9) Would you have given Augusta's note to her husband or hidden it from him like Dean did? Discuss why Dean does this and whether or not she was protecting Maddox. What are the consequences of Dean's actions? Why does Maddox get so angry when he finally reads the letter?

For a complete readers' guide, visit www.hyperionbooks.com

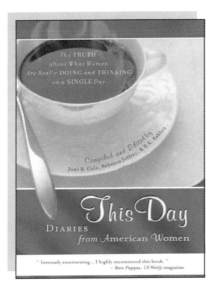

THIS DAY
Diaries from American Women

Editors: **Joni B. Cole,
Rebecca Joffrey, & B.K Rakhra**

Publisher: Beyond Words, 2003

Website: www.beyondword.com

Available in:
Paperback, 304 pages. $15.95
(ISBN 1-58270-102-4)

Subject: Women's Studies/
Personal Challenges (Nonfiction)

Summary

An unprecedented 500 women from across the country unlocked their diaries on one single day. What is a day in the life really like for Miss America, a convicted killer, a star forward for the WNBA, a TV celebrity, a New York Times reporter, the CEO of a corporate icon, a Congresswoman, a young wife and mother with a dying husband, a Grammy-nominated musician, the President of NOW? This Day is a compelling collection of "day diaries" from these women and many others, revealing the truth about what women are actually doing during the course of a single day—and how they really feel about their families, their jobs, and themselves.

Recommended by: Lian Dolan, columnist, *Oprah Magazine*

"What an amazing feat to pull off, capturing a single day from so many fascinating points of view."

Editor Biography

This Day was conceived, compiled, and edited by **Joni B. Cole**, **Rebecca Joffrey**, and **B.K. Rakhra**. Cole is a writer/editor and mom, who co-wrote a business strategy book. Joffrey is an entrepreneur and marketing executive; she and her husband recently had their first baby. Rakhra is a freelance feature writer and full-time fiction writer. The three partners and friends live and work in Vermont.

Topics to Consider

1) Which day diarists did you relate to the most strongly? What was it about these women's lives or attitudes that made you feel a particular connection with them? Were these women overtly similar to yourself or were their circumstances (lifestyle, ethnicity, income level) different from your own?

2) The book's creators arranged for every day diarist to create her day diary on the same day, regardless of whether this was an ordinary or extraordinary day in her life. What value does this bring to the book? How would the book have been different if the participants had been able to choose their own day to create a day diary?

3) How does each woman's attitude shape her day? How does it match the reality of her life? How does attitude shape your day?

4) Many book reviewers and culture commentators claim that in the past several years we have witnessed a memoir explosion. Why has this genre become so popular with readers and writers alike? What are the benefits (and drawbacks) of writers sharing an intimate view of their lives with the general public?

5) A lot of women were surprised to be asked to participate in this book project, initially discounting their lives as "not interesting enough." Why do you think this attitude was so prevalent? Do you think women's voices are marginalized in our society and the media? Does this contribute to a devaluing of women's real-life experiences?

6) Did you notice any common themes—or were you able to draw any general conclusions—about women as a gender or about American culture?

7) After reading these day diaries, do you think it would be of value for you to take stock of a single day in your life? What might you learn about how you really spend your time, your attitude as you go through your day, and the things you like and don't like about your life?

8) How did reading these day diaries change (or reinforce) your perspective about your own life? If you could read a day diary from any woman, whose day diary would you love to read?

For more information, visit www.thisdayinthelife.com

THE VIRGIN'S KNOT

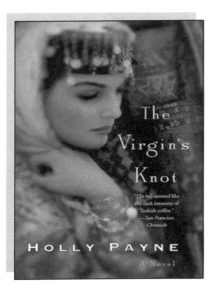

Author: **Holly Payne**

Publisher: Plume Books, 2003

Website: www.penguin.com

Available in:
Paperback, 320 pages. $14.00
(ISBN 0-452-28445-7)

Subject: Culture & World Issues/
Identity/Women's Studies (Fiction)

Summary

She is called Nurdane, the famed weaver of Mavisu. From her remote mountain village in southwestern Turkey, she creates dowries for young brides: dazzling rugs, marvels of shape and color, texture and light. But it is her hands—the hands of an artist, and a virgin—that hold the essence of her mystery. An extraordinary series of events drives Nurdane to question the limitations of her faith and culture as she is caught between remaining pure in body and spirit...or risking everything for love. A novel imbued with the history and lore of Turkish culture and tradition, *The Virgin's Knot* chronicles a young woman's journey from innocence to knowledge, from loneliness to love.

Recommended by: *The San Francisco Chronicle*

"[To be] savored like the dark intensity of Turkish coffee."

Author Biography

Holly Payne teaches screenwriting at the Academy of Art College in San Francisco. She received her M.F.A. from the University of Southern California Master of Professional Writing Program in Los Angeles. She lives in San Francisco, California, where she is at work on her second novel. For more, visit **www.holly-payne.com.**

Topics to Consider

1) What is the significance of Ali pushing Nurdane to do the work of Allah? What kind of burden does he put on Nurdane? Is Ali trying to protect Nurdane or benefit from her talents?

2) Why doesn't Nurdane immediately tell her father about the thieves? What was she trying to protect? How did the experience make her feel about herself? What does Nurdane's silence teach us about her character?

3) What role does Muammer play in Nurdane's life? How does Muammer help her and why? Is he genuinely concerned or just nosy?

4) What are the similarities between Ayse and Nurdane? What are the differences? How are all of the women in Mavisu linked by tradition?

5) What is Hennessy hoping to find in Mavisu? Does he find what he is looking for? How does Nurdane help him to find it?

6) What motivates Adam's love for Nurdane? Does Nurdane find Adam's medical help useful?

7) How does Hennessey's gesture in picking up the scarf when he first meets Nurdane challenge the way men and women interact in a traditional Islamic society?

8) Why did Nurdane bury the razor blade that she found in the woods with Muammer? Why did this make Muammer nervous? Is Nurdane superstitious?

9) Despite the sexual innuendoes, what is the true reward that Nurdane receives by leading Hennessy into the cave?

For additional discussion topics, visit www.penguin.com

WAITING FOR APRIL

Author: Scott M. Morris

Publisher: Algonquin Books, 2003

Website: www.algonquin.com

Available in:
Hardcover, 340 pages. $24.95
(ISBN 1-565-12370-0)

Subject: Family/
Intrigue (Fiction)

Summary

On a stormy night in 1965, a man carrying a suitcase holding army discharge papers and a Bronze Star strode into the little town of Citrus, Florida, and changed everything. He called himself Sanders Collier and said he was the son of a prominent family of South Carolina gentry. He was handsome and cunning, and people believed him. Within a few years he would be dead, shot in what would always be called a hunting accident. Who was hunting what was never clear to his son, left behind to make sense of a town split apart by the things his father had done. But when Roy grows into the spitting image of his father, the unspoken agreement to keep buried the old resentments about the past comes undone. What follows for this family is the unraveling of every lie, half-truth, self-delusion, and wishful thought on which they had built their lives since the arrival of Sanders Collier, and Roy's ultimate understanding of what happened the night his father died.

Recommended by: Associated Press

"Morris' strength is in his characters. He manages to handle them with both sensitivity and humor."

Author Biography

Scott M. Morris is a frequent contributor to the *Los Angeles Times*, the *Wall Street Journal*, and the *Oxford American*, among others. He teaches at the University of Mississippi in Oxford, and is the author of the acclaimed debut novel *The Total View of Taftly*.

Topics to Consider

1) In what ways is Roy like his father, Sanders Collier? In what ways is he different? In what ways does Roy's mother encourage Roy to be more like his father?

2) Discuss the dynamic in the marriage of Roy's parents.

3) Roy has a number of potential role models in the novel. Identify each of these and explain what he learns from each of them, both negatively and positively.

4) Discuss the meaning of the title. Who is waiting for April in the town, and what is it that they want of her? How much of this has to do with who April really is, and how much has to do with what people want to see in her?

5) Discuss Roy's relationship with Lori-Anne. How is it different from his relationship to April? Which relationship is more real? Which woman is more respected for who she is?

6) What do you think is more devastating to Roy: what he learns about his father, or what he learns about his mother?

7) As Stearns' account reveals, so much of our understanding of history is shaped by who's doing the telling. Describe the many versions of history that the novel provides, and discuss the difficulty of deciding whose version to fully believe. What stake do we have in our stories and histories, whether true or untrue?

8) April is in many ways characterized as an ideal woman. But in what respect is April responsible for the turn of events in the book, in relation to Roy?

9) What is the significance of Roy's father's true identity? What does this say about issues of identity for everyone in the book but especially Roy, April, June?

10) Morris uses Christian imagery throughout, from scenes set at Christmas, to references to Easter and walking on water, and so on. What is the function of this imagery in relation to larger themes in the book?

THE WAY THE CROW FLIES

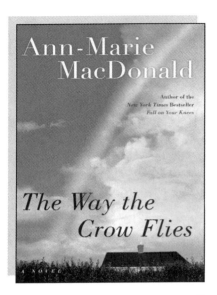

Author: **Ann-Marie MacDonald**

Publisher: HarperCollins, 10/2003

Website: www.harpercollins.com

Available in:
Hardcover, 736 pages. $26.95
(ISBN 0-06-057895-5)

Subject: Intrigue (Fiction)

Summary

For Madeleine McCarthy, high-spirited and eight years old, her family's posting to a quiet air force base near the Canadian-American border is at first welcome, secure as she is in the love of her beautiful mother, and unaware that her father, Jack, is caught up in his own web of secrets. The base is host to some intriguing inhabitants, including the unconventional Froehlich family, and the odd Mr. March whose power over the children is a secret burden that they carry. Soon after the McCarthy's move tragedy strikes, and a very local murder intersects with global forces, binding the participants for life. As the tension builds, Jack must decide where his loyalties lie, and Madeleine learns about the ambiguity of human morality—a lesson she will only begin to understand when she carries her quest for the truth, and the killer, into adulthood twenty years later.

Recommended by: *The New York Times Book Review*

"This resonant first novel...[has] a mythic quality that allows dark secrets to be gracefully and chillingly revealed."

Author Biography

Novelist and dramatist **Ann-Marie MacDonald** is the author of the international bestselling and award-winning novel *Fall On Your Knees*. She also won the Governor General's Award for Drama and the Canadian Author's Award for Fiction. She lives in Toronto.

Topics to Consider

1) How does the author demonstrate the time period throughout the story?

2) Through brief passages preceding some chapters, MacDonald offers the reader small tidbits of information pertaining to the story that would otherwise remain unknown. Why do you think the author uses this narrative technique?

3) In what ways do you feel Madeline grows and changes throughout the novel?

4) There are many different definitions of "home" in this novel. What does "home" mean to each character and how does the definition change with time?

5) How do you think Madeleine's perspective of that time has changed now that she has aged and her innocence and optimism have faded?

6) Madeleine and her father are both keeping secrets about key events in the book. What, if any, parallels can you see between the secrets they are keeping?

7) Does Jack's top-secret government position absolve him of the responsibility of testifying for the man who is wrongly accused of murder? Does this fall under the same category as soldiers who renounce guilt for their actions because they were "just following orders"?

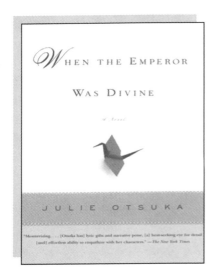

WHEN THE EMPEROR WAS DIVINE

Author: Julie Otsuka

Publisher: Anchor Books, 2003

Website:
www.readinggroupcenter.com

Available in:
Paperback, 160 pages. $9.95
(ISBN 0-385-72181-1)

Subject: History/Family/
Culture & World Issues (Fiction)

Summary

A woman reads a sign in a post office window. It is Berkeley, California, the spring of 1942. Pearl Harbor has been attacked, the war is on, and though the precise message on the sign is not revealed, its impact on the woman who reads it is immediate and profound. It is, in many ways she cannot yet foresee, a sign of things to come. She readies herself and her two young children for a journey that will take them to the high desert plains of Utah. They travel by train and gradually the reader discovers that all on board are Japanese American, and that their destination is an internment camp where they will be imprisoned "for their own safety" until the war is over. This novel reveals the dark underside of a moment in American history that, until now, has been left largely unexplored in American fiction.

Recommended by: *The New York Times*

"Mesmerizing.... [Otsuka has] lyric gifts and narrative poise, [a] heat-seeking eye for detail [and] effortless ability to empathize with her characters."

Author Biography

Julie Otsuka was born in Palo Alto and studied art at Yale University. After pursuing a career as a painter, she turned to fiction at age 30. One of her short stories was included in Scribner's *Best of the Fiction Workshops* 1998, edited by Carol Shields. *When the Emperor Was Divine* is her first novel.

Topics to Consider

1) In what ways does the novel deepen our existing knowledge of this historical period? What does it give readers that a straightforward historical investigation cannot?

2) Otsuka skillfully places subtle but significant details in her narrative. How do these details, and others like them, point to larger meanings in the novel?

3) Why does Otsuka refer to her characters as "the woman," "the girl," "the boy," and "the father," rather than giving them names? How does this lack of specific identities affect the reader's relationship to the characters?

4) When the boy wonders why he's in the camp, he worries that "he'd done something horribly, terribly wrong.... It could be anything" [p. 57]. What does this reveal about the damaging effects of racism on children? What does it reveal about the way children try to make sense of their experience?

5) Much of *When the Emperor Was Divine* is told in short, episodic, loosely connected scenes—images, conversations, memories, dreams, and so on—that move between past and present and alternate points of view between the mother, daughter, and son. Why has Otsuka chosen to structure her narrative in this way? What effects does it allow her to achieve?

6) After the father returns home, he never once discusses the years he'd been away, and his children don't ask. Why would their father remain silent about such an important experience? In what ways does the novel fight against this desire to forget?

7) The mother is denied work because being a Japanese American might "upset the other employees" or offend the customers. What strengths does she exhibit throughout her ordeal?

8) Who is speaking in the final chapter? Is the speech entirely ironic? Why has Otsuka chosen to end the novel in this way? What does the confession imply about our ability to separate out the "enemy," the "other," in our midst?

For a complete Reading Group Guide,
visit www.readinggroupcenter.com

THE WHITE

Author: Deborah Larsen

Publisher: Vintage Books, 2003

Website:
www.readinggroupcenter.com

Available in:
Paperback, 240 pages. $12.95
(ISBN 0-375-71289-5)

Subject: History/
Identity (Fiction)

Summary

In the spring of 1758 Mary Jemison and her family were taken captive by a Shawnee raiding party near Gettysburg, Pennsylvania. While the rest of her family was killed by the Shawnee, Mary was chosen for adoption by a Seneca family in exchange for a son of theirs who had been killed by whites. Mary lived among the Indians for the rest of her life, bore children to two husbands, and even when offered the chance to return to white society chose to remain with the Seneca. Deborah Larsen uses Mary Jemison's story as the basis for an elegant and riveting novel, bringing to vivid life not only an extraordinary woman but also a whole cultural conflict between natives and white settlers in the early decades of the American nation.

Recommended by: *The New York Times*

"Riveting...lyrical.... An indelible portrait of a remarkable woman.... A brutal and beautiful novel."

Author Biography

Deborah Larsen grew up in St. Paul, MN, and now lives with her husband in Pennsylvania, where she teaches creative writing at Gettysburg College. Her collection of poetry, "Stitching Porcelain," was published in 1991, and her poems and short stories have appeared in *The Nation, The Yale Review,* and *The New Yorker,* among other publications. She has been a Wallace Stegner Fellow at Stanford and a Wallace Stevens Fellow at Yale. *The White* is her first novel.

Topics to Consider

1) Why do the Shawnee decide to keep Mary as a captive, and to kill the rest of her family? Why, in the midst of all this, does she resent her father so much? Does Mary show more maturity of judgment than her father does? Does Mary's wish to die, soon after her family is killed, differ from the passivity she so scorned in her father?

2) For a time Mary enters a period that can be interpreted as a state of severe depression. How does Larsen approach psychology as a critical element in her reconstruction of the character of Mary Jemison? How does the author use imagery and lyricism to convey these ideas?

3) How do ceremonies demonstrate the Indians' ideas about human emotion, and the necessity of keeping destructive spirits at bay?

4) After Mary encounters an Englishwoman at Fort Pitt and thinks about the woman's family [pp. 37–39], she quotes lines from the Scriptures to herself for days afterwards; are these quotations the truth of her experience? Are they necessary for her as she mourns for herself and her family?

5) How do Mary's Indian sisters respond to her state of despondency? How does the episode in which Mary cuts her hand and speaks the word "blood" change things for her, and change her relationship with Slight Wind? Is there a necessary movement from self-absorption to objectivity in this episode?

6) How does Larsen distinguish between the differing attitudes of Indians and whites toward nature and the land, to shared work and ideas of community? In early-19th century society, is it surprising to find Mary befriending ex-slaves, and Indians living side by side with whites?

7) To what degree does the novel suggest that the white colonists are responsible for the disintegration of Indian tribal life and traditions? Who, for instance, is to blame for the deaths of Mary's sons? How satisfying is the novel's ending, with Mary owning her own land, living a peaceful life surrounded by the remaining members of her Indian family?

For a complete Reading Group Guide,
visit www.readinggroupcenter.com

WHITE APPLES

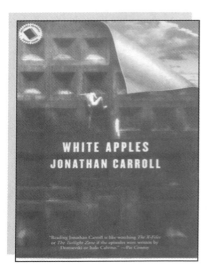

Author: **Jonathan Carroll**

Publisher: Tor Books, 2003

Website: www.tor.com

Available in:
Paperback, 304 pages. $13.95
(ISBN 0-765-30401-5)

Subject: Identity/
Intrigue (Fiction)

Summary

Vincent Ettrich, a genial philanderer, discovers that he has died and come back to life, but he has no idea why, or what the experience was like. Pushed and prodded by peculiar omens and personalities, he gradually learns that he was brought back by his one true love, Isabelle, because she is pregnant with their child—a child who, if raised correctly, will play a crucial role in saving the cosmic mosaic that is the universe. But to be brought up right, he must be educated by his father. Specifically, he must be taught what Ettrich learned on the other side—if only Ettrich can remember it!

Recommended by: Neil Gaiman, author of *Coraline*

"Jonathan Carroll has the magic. He'll lend you his eyes, and you'll never see the world in quite the same way again."

Author Biography

Jonathan Carroll, known for his unusual characters and fantastical events, is the author of thirteen novels, the most recent of which is *The Wooden Sea*. After earning a Masters Degree from the University of Virginia, Carroll became an English teacher and worked at various schools in the U.S. before moving to Vienna, Austria to teach at the American International School, where he is still teaching today.

Topics to Consider

1) Among the central themes of *White Apples* are transition and transformation. Such transitions include that of life to death, ignorance to enlightenment, and changes in personal growth and responsibility. How are these transformations manifested in Vincent, Isabelle, and Bruno? Which seems to have the most dramatic impact upon each character?

2) How do the characters' personality traits influence their actions and reactions throughout the story?

3) Discuss the idea of the great Mosaic. How does it work as a religious philosophy?

4) The scene at the zoo is one of the most powerful and disturbing in the book. In it, the zoo animals have willingly accepted their captivity to serve as guardians of humanity. How does this define the place of humans in the universal pecking order?

5) Describe how animals are portrayed throughout the novel and their importance to the story. Does Carroll's presentation of animal characteristics strike you as fair?

6) Coco Hallis compares Purgatory to a school where we are taught the secrets of life and have the opportunity to review the choices we made during life. How does this compare to other major religious philosophies?

7) Many times in love stories, the hero and heroine are so perfectly fitted that they have no choice but to fall in love. In real life, this is hardly the case. Discuss love in relation to Vincent and Isabelle. How did their own imperfection strengthen their love?

8) What roles do children play in the novel? Are the portrayals of Anjo, Jack, and the children at the zoo realistic or symbolic in nature?

9) Which characters in *White Apples* do you feel are the most interesting? Which are the most realistic? How do you think you would react to the news of your own death and resurrection?

***For additional topics and information,
visit www.jonathancarroll.com***

WINTERING
A Novel of Sylvia Plath

Author: Kate Moses

Publisher: Anchor Books, 2003

Website:
www.readinggroupcenter.com

Available in:
Paperback, 336 pages. $13.00
(ISBN 1-4000-3500-7)

Subject: Biography (Fiction)

Summary

In this novel, Kate Moses re-creates Sylvia Plath's last months, weaving in the background of her life before she met Ted Hughes through to the disintegration of their relationship and the burst of creativity this triggered. It is inspired by Plath's original ordering and selection of the poems in *Ariel*—which begins with the word 'love' and ends with 'spring'—a mythic narrative of defiant survival quite different from the chronological version edited by Hughes. At *Wintering's* heart, though, lie the two weeks in December 1962 when Plath finds herself still alone and grief-stricken, despite all her determined hope. With empathy and grace, Moses captures her poignant and courageous struggle to confront not only her future as a woman, an artist, and a mother, but also the unbanished demons of her past.

Recommended by: *The New York Times Book Review*

"Beautiful and moving.... A novel about ambition, motherhood, identity, and love."

Author Biography

Kate Moses has worked as an editor in publishing and as literary director at San Francisco's Intersection for the Arts. With Camille Peri, she co-edited the American Book Award–winning anthology *Mothers Who Think.* She lives in San Francisco with her husband and their two children.

Topics to Consider

1) A novel about an actual historical figure is different from most works of fiction. What is the relationship of fiction to fact, especially as it relates to the experience of reading *Wintering?*

2) Is *Wintering* meant to stand alone as a novel, or is it meant to stand in necessary relation to Plath's poetry, her journals, her biographies, etc.? What prior knowledge of the subject, if any, does the novel presuppose on the part of the reader?

3) Does it seem true that the breakup of her marriage, with all its grief and anger, was the precipitating cause of Plath's extraordinary breakthrough? If so, what does this suggest about the nature of her gift?

4) Does the novel show Plath in a state of suicidal despair? Do you think her suicide was inevitable? Do you think Plath thought that was the only course of action available to her?

5) What does Court Green symbolize for Sylvia, with its ancient grounds, daffodils, and apple trees?

6) *Wintering* is an imaginative reconstruction of Sylvia Plath's life during a time of extreme stress and creativity; her journals from this period were destroyed by Ted Hughes. Given this fact, does *Wintering* stand as a useful, even necessary attempt to recreate the aspects of Plath's experience now lost from the historical record?

7) Comment on the novel's structure, particularly on Moses's practice of dating each chapter. Why might Moses have decided to end the novel on December 29, 1962, rather than on February 11, 1963, the day of Plath's death? What is the tone of the final chapter?

8) What aspects of Plath's life and state of mind, as depicted by Moses, pull the reader most powerfully into sympathy with her plight?

For a complete reading group guide,
visit www.readinggroupcenter.com

Want to talk to you favorite author?

Choose one of the books below as the next book for your reading group and the author can be a part of your group's discussion

---

City of Your Final Destination, **by Peter Cameron**
"Delightful, unexpected, magical, romantic."—*USA Today*

Early From the Dance, **by David Payne**
"Brilliant...A defining voice for his generation."—*The Boston Globe*

Sugar, **by Bernice McFadden**
"One of the most compelling and thought-provoking novels
I've read in years."—Terry McMillian

The Captain's Wife, **by Douglas Kelley**
"A splendid contribution to recent literature."
—*Arkansas Democrat Gazette*

The Virgin's Knot, **by Holly Payne**
"[To be] savored like the dark intensity of Turkish coffee."
—*San Francisco Chronicle*

Lydia Cassatt Reading the Morning Paper, **by Harriet Scott Chessman**
"This flowing and lyrical novel...captures a bit of Paris of the time."
—Alan Cheuse, NPR's *All Things Considered*

Souls of My Brothers, **edited by Dawn Marie Daniels and Candace Sandy**
"Riveting, revealing, and reflective."
—Les Brown, motivational speaker/author

Sister Noon, **by Karen Joy Fowler**
"No contemporary writer creates characters more appealing, or examines them
with greater acuity and forgiveness."—Michael Chabon

To invite one of these authors to join your group via phone,
E-mail: Plume.Marketing@us.penguingroup.com
or
Fax: (212) 366-2815, Attn: Plume Marketing

Please include the day of the week and time your book group meets

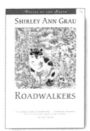

"...Rich in texture, abundant in
human connection, alive with
color, spirit, and grace.
A must-read book for knitting
neophytes and devotees alike."

–Bernadette Murphy
author of *Zen and the Art of Knitting*

Published by Tarcher/Penguin
a member of Penguin Group (USA) Inc.
ISBN 1-58542-210-X
Reading Guide Available

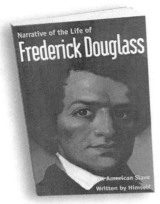

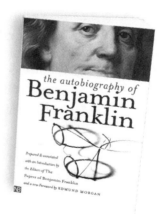

RESOURCES

The Internet

Reading Group Choices Online — guides available from major publishers and independent presses that can be printed directly from the site: www.readinggroupchoices.com

For new book information, reading lists, book news and literary events, visit ReadingGroupGuides.com, generousbooks.com, BookSpot.com, and BookMuse.com. Looking for reading guides for children? Visit KidsReads.com.

Publisher Web Sites — Find additional topics for discussion, special offers for book groups, and other titles of interest.

Algonquin Books of Chapel Hill — *algonquin.com*
Anchor Books — *readinggroupcenter.com*
Back Bay Books — *twbookmark.com*
Ballantine Books — *ballantinebooks.com/BRC*
Beagle Bay Books — *beaglebay.com*
Beagle Bay Books — *beaglebay.com*
Beyond Words — *beyondword.com*
Coffee House Press — *coffeehousepress.org*
Doubleday Books — *doubleday.com*
HarperCollins — *harpercollins.com*
Hyperion Books — *hyperionbooks.com*
Knopf Books — *aaknopf.com*
Little, Brown & Co. — *twbookmark.com*
Middleway Press — *middlewaypress.org*
Penguin Putnam — *penguinputnam.com/guides*
Picador — *picadorusa.com*
Plume Books — *penguin.com*
Random House — *randomhouse.com*
Rodale Books — *rodale.com*
Tor Books — *tor.com*
Vintage Books — *readinggroupcenter.com*
Warner Books — *twbookmark.com*
Yale University Press — *yalebooks.com*

Newsletters and Book Lists

BookWomen: A Readers' Community for Those Who Love Women's Words, a bimonthly "bookletter" published by the Minnesota Women's Press. Includes recommendations, news about the book world, and articles for and about women readers and writers. Subscription: $24/yr. (6 issues). Contact: books@womenspress.com or
Minnesota Women's Press
771 Raymond Ave.
St. Paul, MN 55114
(651) 646-3968

Reverberations News Journal, Rachel Jacobsohn's publication of the Association of Book Group Readers and Leaders. Annual membership including subscription is $20. Contact: rachelj@attbi.com

Books & Journals

Bibliotherapy: The Girl's Guide to Books for Every Phase of Our Lives by Nancy Peske and Beverly West. Published by DTP, ISBN 0-4405-0897-5, $13.95.

The Book Group Book: A Thoughtful Guide to Forming and Enjoying a Stimulating Book Discussion Group. Edited by Ellen Slezak and Margaret Eleanor Atwood. Published by Chicago Review Press, ISBN 1-5565-2412-9, $14.95.

Circles of Sisterhood: A Book Discussion Group Guide for Women of Color by Pat Neblett. Published by Writers & Readers, ISBN 0-8631-6245-2, $14.

Contemporary Multi-Ethnic Novels by Women Coming of Age Together in the New America by Rochelle Holt, Ph.D. Published by Thanks Be to Grandmother Winifred Foundation, $5 + SASE (6" by 8"). Write to 15223 Coral Isle Ct., Ft. Myers, FL 33919.

Family Book Sharing Groups: Start One in Your Neighborhood! By Marjorie R. Simic with Eleanor C. MacFarlane. Published by the Family Literacy Center, 1-8837-9011-5, $6.95.

Literature Circles: Voice and Choice in Book Clubs and Reading Groups by Harvey Daniels. Published by Stenhouse Publishers, ISBN 1-5711-0333-3, $22.50.

Minnesota Women's Press Great Books. An annotated listing of 236 books by women authors chosen by over 3,000 women participating in Minnesota Women's Press Book Groups in the past 13 years. $10.95 + $2 s/h. (612) 646-3968.

The Mother-Daughter Book Club: How Ten Busy Mothers and Daughters Came Together to Talk, Laugh and Learn Through Their Love of Reading by Shireen Dodson and Teresa Barker. Published by HarperCollins, ISBN 0-0609-5242-3, $14.

The Readers' Choice: 200 Book Club Favorites by Victoria McMains. Published by Wm. Morrow, ISBN 0-6881-7435-3, $14.

The Reading Group Book: The Complete Guide to Starting and Sustaining a Reading Group by David Laskin and Holly Hughes. Published by Plume, ISBN 0-452-27201-7, $11.95.

The Reading Group Handbook: Everything You Need to Know to Start Your Own Book Club by Rachel Jacobsohn. Published by Hyperion, ISBN 0-786-88324-3, $12.95.

Reading Group Journal: Notes in the Margin by Martha Burns and Alice Dillon. Published by Abbeville Press, ISBN 0-7892-0586-6, $16.95.

The Reading List: Contemporary Fiction, A Critical Guide to the Complete Works of 125 Authors. Edited by David Rubel. Published by Owl Books, ISBN 0-805055-27-4, $17.

Reading to Heal: A Reading Group Strategy for Better Health by Diane Dawber. Published by Quarry Press, ISBN 1-5508-2229-2, $9.95.

Talking About Books: A Step-by-Step Guide for Participating in a Book Discussion Group by Marcia Fineman. Published by Talking About Books, ISBN 0-9661-5670-6, $15.

Talking About Books: Literature Discussion Groups in K-8 Classrooms by Kathy Short. Published by Heinemann, ISBN 0-3250-0073-5, $24.

What to Read: The Essential Guide for Reading Group Members and Other Book Lovers by Mickey Pearlman. Published by HarperCollins, ISBN 0-0609-5313-6, $14.

A Year of Reading: A Month-By-Month Guide to Classics and Crowd-Pleasers for You or Your Book Group by H. E. Ellington and Jane Freimiller. Published by Sourcebooks, ISBN 1-5707-1935-7, $14.95.

INDEX BY SUBJECT/INTEREST AREA

WHAT OTHER GROUPS HAVE READ — AND ENJOYED

Early in the year, we asked book groups on **Reading Group Choices Online** to tell us about the books they read and discussed during the previous year that they enjoyed most. It's always interesting to see the hundreds of titles that get recommended—and which ones appear in the top 20.

What were your favorites of 2003?

Visit us online and with your entry, you'll have the chance to receive books for each person in your group (compliments of one of our publishing partners) and a check for $75 to cater one of your next meetings.

Register January 1 — March 31, 2004
At www.readinggroupchoices.com

BOOK GROUP FAVORITES FROM 2002

1) ***Girl With a Pearl Earring*** by Tracy Chevalier (Plume)
2) ***The Red Tent*** by Anita Diamant (Picador USA)
3) ***The Lovely Bones*** by Alice Sebold (Little Brown)
4) ***Empire Falls*** by Richard Russo (Vintage)
5) ***Peace Like a River*** by Leif Enger (Grove)
6) ***Seabiscuit*** by Laura Hillenbrand (Ballantine)
7) ***Bel Canto*** by Ann Patchett (HarperPerennial)
8) ***John Adams*** by David McCullough (Simon & Schuster)
9) ***Girl in Hyacinth Blue*** by Susan Vreeland (Penguin)
10) ***The Poisonwood Bible*** by Barbara Kingsolver (HarperPerennial)
11) ***Pope Joan*** by Donna Woolfolk Cross (Ballantine)
12) ***To Kill a Mockingbird*** by Harper Lee (Warner & HarperCollins)
13) ***Big Stone Gap*** by Adriana Trigiani (Ballantine)
14) ***The Bonesetter's Daughter*** by Amy Tan (Ballantine)
15) ***Jim the Boy*** by Tony Earley (Back Bay)
16) ***The Jew Store*** by Stella Suberman (Algonquin)
17) ***Ahab's Wife*** by Sena Jeter Naslund (HarperPerennial)
18) ***The Secret Life of Bees*** by Sue Monk Kidd (Penguin)
19) ***A Fine Balance*** by Rohinton Mistry (Vintage)
20) ***Hanna's Daughters*** by Marianne Fredriksson (Ballantine)